Contents

Acknowledgements

To every single person who has contributed and supported my journey, I truly thank you from the bottom of my heart. To everyone mentioned in this book and to those who have contributed along the way, please know that your support and endeavours have meant so much to me. To Trevor Dolby, Ajda Vučićević, Becky Millar, Laura Brooke and all at Cornerstone, Penguin Random House, Stephanie Cross, Mervyn Lyn and my manager Abby Newell, who made it possible for me to tell this story in my own words.

Photographic Acknowledgements

- 'Carl, Blueberry and I.' © Birmingham Post Mail
- 'Blueberry was ready for this performance. We both were.' © Alex Livesey/Getty Images
- 'Holy moly!...' © Alex Livesey/Getty Images and © sampics/Getty Images
- 'September brought the 'Our Greatest Team'...' © WPA Pool/Pool/Getty Images
- 'We were invited back to Buckingham Palace...' © WPA Pool/Pool/Getty Images
- 'The most nerve-wracking part of receiving my MBE...' © PA Archive/Press Association Images
- 'Blueberry and I are not machines...' © Friso Gentsch/ DPA Picture Alliance/Alamy Stock Photo

1

A Family Affair

PEOPLE OFTEN ASK me if dressage horses dance by themselves. 'Are you just sitting there steering?' they say. 'Because I've watched you and I can't see how you're doing it.'

It's a question I love, because if it doesn't look like I'm doing anything then I'm doing something right. Dressage is all about harmony: having a relationship with your horse where it has confidence in you so that everything you do together looks effortless and easy, like it's all happening by magic. But I can tell you now, there wasn't a whole lot of harmony at the beginning.

The first time I remember sitting on a horse I must have been three or four years old. She was called Sovereign and she was dark beige with white socks and a little white blaze down her face. We were in the field at the back of our house in Hoddesdon, Hertfordshire and my mum was trying to teach me, but this naughty little pony just would not stop putting her head down to eat grass.

Horses were my mum Jane's passion. She'd evented and had a good career as a show jumper before she got pregnant with my sister Emma-Jayne, who was born in 1982. Then I came along in 1985, followed by my brother Charles in 1986. Mum carried on competing for a bit after we were born, but we ended up being too much of a distraction: we'd cry for her when she was in the ring, and when she was driving to shows

1

we'd need her to stop the horsebox all the time so we could go for a wee.

Mum still had a few horses while we were little and when she was mucking them out in the mornings we'd be desperately trying to get on their backs. Mum would throw us up on top to shut us up and we'd sit there, clinging onto their rugs, clicking our tongues and trying to gee them up while she carried on working. I never wanted to get down when she'd finished – she literally had to peel me off.

Mum must have been ready to tear her hair out, watching me trying to ride Sovereign. 'Give her a kick! Give her a kick!' she kept yelling, but I was so tiny my legs didn't even reach her sides and were just banging up and down on the saddle. I sat there flapping away and eventually Mum lost it completely and came over and shooed us into a trot. Off we'd go for a couple of strides, then the next minute Sovereign's head was back down and she'd start eating again. No matter what I did, I just could not get her to move.

Looking back, it wasn't the greatest start to my career, but even then horses were how I wanted to spend every minute of every day. At school I'd sit at my desk hating every second and trying to work out how many years of it I'd got left: it wasn't going to help me ride better, so for me there wasn't any point in being there. My elder sister was the naughty one who played truant, but I was always too scared of getting into trouble in case Mum banned me from riding. I couldn't pretend I was too ill for school, either: 'Oh, no, if you can ride your ponies, you're perfectly fine. Get your uniform on and hurry up.'

How different would it have been if my maternal grandmother had got her way and Mum had been a dancer? My nan was originally a dressmaker and her marriage to my granddad was the second time for both of them. Mum's stepsister was a professional dancer with a job on *The Sooty Show*, but Mum (as she'll say herself) was not cut out to be on the stage, even though she was sent to stage school.

Her dad had his own business making light fittings and was very successful in his younger years. His own father had bought a house in Sintra, Portugal in the 1950s, and during the summer my great-grandfather came back to England to look after the family business while my nan and granddad took my mum, her brother and step-siblings to Portugal on holiday.

My granddad was very generous with his money, and much more supportive of my mum's equestrian interests than my nan was. One year when they were on holiday he finally caved in and bought my mum a horse, and then when they got home he bought her another so she had one to ride in England as well. What nobody knew was that the Portuguese horse was in foal, so it wasn't long before there were three. Eventually, my granddad decided the amount of money he was spending on livery was ridiculous and he might as well just buy a house with stables. My nan found a derelict farm near Broxbourne in Hertfordshire and they ended up converting it into one of the best yards in the area, to the point where a very important visitor came to stay: Red Rum.

Apparently, Mum was out hacking one afternoon when she was stopped by a passing car. The driver was an assistant to 'Ginger' McCain, who had famously trained Red Rum to three Grand National victories in the 1970s. It turned out that Red Rum, by then retired from racing, was opening the Hoddesdon and Broxbourne Carnival that year and needed somewhere to stay locally. Mum didn't hesitate to recommend her home, White

Stubbs Farm, so along came Red Rum for a couple of nights – the first superstar horse in the family.

My mum had known my dad, Ian, most of her life. The Dujardins had played a big part in the medieval cotton industry in France, but Dad was born in Enfield, Greater London, not far from where my mum's parents were living. They were childhood sweethearts growing up, and when my grandparents sold their house to move to White Stubbs Farm, it was Ian's parents who bought it. Dad had his own packaging company when he married Mum in 1981, and for a while they lived in Cheshunt, Hertfordshire, but when I was about nine months old we moved to The Round House, which had eight stables and a proper outdoor school.

It was after we'd moved there that Mum decided to get into show ponies. She wasn't the type of person who could just have horses as a hobby, and she knew that in the showing world kids could compete from the age of two.

One of the first shows I can remember was a lead-rein class on my little chestnut, Toy Grenadier, when I was four. Because my sister was older she'd already done all her lead reins, which drove me crazy, and Mum and I would argue about it all the time.

'I don't want to be on the lead! I want to do what Emma-Jayne's doing!'

'You have to be on the lead, Charlotte, that's why it's a lead-rein class.'

I couldn't wait until the moment at the end when she'd let me off so I could go for a ride round the car park on my own.

Being too small to tack up my own pony was another thing that really used to annoy me: even when I was strong enough to pick up the saddle, I couldn't always find something to stand on so I could reach. I was very proud when I finally managed to do it, because until then I'd always had to watch Mum, and being able to do what she was doing made me feel like such a grown up.

We weren't allowed to muck around on the show ponies at home, but when I was three or four Mum and Dad bought us a couple of little black hairy Shetlands called Sally and Jo-Jo. Sally came all wrapped up with a massive red ribbon round her tummy, and my sister and I would fight over who got stuck riding her because Jo-Jo was really good, whereas Sally would stop, buck and then fling you clean off. We'd have races across the field and down to the river to see who could go the fastest, and one of us would always end up on the ground either because we'd been bucked off or gone flying over our pony's head when it stopped to eat grass.

One day, we decided that we wanted to drive Sally like a carthorse. We'd seen my mum driving horses at White Stubbs Farm and although we didn't have a cart we did have a silver garden wheelbarrow. We put a milk crate in it to sit on, then tied Sally to the handles with some rope round her belly and got her to tow us round the place. It was absolutely brilliant, but you can imagine what your mum's going to say when she comes out of the house and sees you doing that.

'What the *hell* do you think you're doing?!'

All three of us were naughty kids. When my brother was slightly older my parents bought him a quad bike and my dad put some kind of speed-limiting device on the throttle for safety. As soon as Dad wasn't around we worked out how to get it off, then we'd all take turns at going flat-out round the field and fit the control back on when we'd finished so he'd never know.

When we went to shows Charles would sometimes bring his quad along in the back of the lorry. He was less into ponies and more into boy stuff like tractors and motorbikes and fishing, although he was actually quite a good rider when my sister and I managed to get him to do it. The only problem was if his pony cantered and went too fast, because then he'd jump off. He called himself Superman because he'd fly through the air and do a tumble in the sand – if he was going to have to make an exit, bless him, he at least wanted it to be a planned one.

One thing my brother did like getting involved in was making jumps. Although we had a school we had nothing to jump over, so we'd make fences out of anything we could find: milk crates, canisters, logs, bales of straw – you name it, we'd jump it. We'd build it all up as high as we could and when we weren't jumping the horses, we were jumping the dogs – Blitz, who was a pointer; Rugby; Chalkie, who was a Westie; and Jack and Russell, who were self-explanatory. It was all good fun setting everything up but not so much fun putting it away, and of course that was when Charles could never be found.

Another of my brother's loves was his Carolina corn snake, which I was interested in, too: I thought it was quite an educational experience watching the way it could shed its skin in one piece. I even liked feeding it insects, which is just disgusting to think about now, so I'm not surprised that one friend of ours, Wendy Hiard, wouldn't even set foot in our house until she knew the snake was locked in its cage. Obviously, the evening it went missing was an evening when she was round.

We hunted for it absolutely everywhere we could think of: in the cupboards, under the sofa, in the cutlery drawers. Then someone looked up and there it was, twined all round the curtain rail. Poor Wendy screamed the place down. It was great entertainment for the night.

Most weeks, we'd go and visit my nan at White Stubbs Farm, which I always used to enjoy. She'd give us pocket money and take us to the Jolly Waggoner pub for scampi and chips in a basket and generally do all the kinds of things nans do. Visits were harder for my mum because Nan could be quite difficult and after she and Granddad got divorced in the early eighties she also drank quite a lot. When we went to visit her Mum was always trying to tidy and clean the house up a bit, and it must have had an impact on us kids because none of us drink much now. At the time we didn't think about it, though: there was a bar in the house and we'd often pretend to be grown-ups and pour each other Cokes, but we usually spent more time in the yard seeing the liveries than in the house with our nan.

Some of the best times we had together as a family were weekends out hacking with the Dockleys. Paul Dockley was a police officer, and a former boyfriend of Mum's. They had a son who was Emma-Jayne's age and a daughter a bit younger than Charles, and so we gave Jo-Jo the Shetland to them when we grew out of her.

We'd box the ponies up to a village somewhere, and Paul and Wendy would lead their children while my sister and I would ride a couple of our show ponies. My mum and dad would walk and Charles would be on his pushbike. We'd go for miles like this until we came to a pub. Then we'd stop, tie the ponies up and have sandwiches, crisps and Coke out of the bottle – I loved that bit – hack back and drive home again.

One day when we were out we had to cross a ford. The water that the cars drove through was quite shallow, but on either side it was deeper. Right, I thought, I'm taking Dylan in there.

Dylan was a steel grey Welsh Section A with a mane down to his shoulders. He looked like a rocking horse, but he was a real pain to keep clean: before shows we'd have to put his tail in a bag to stop him messing down it and every time you took him out for a hack he'd come back filthy. Anyway, I got him in the water and he started pawing and digging away. I was laughing because water was splashing everywhere, everyone else was laughing while they watched us, but then the next moment Dylan was getting down to roll with me. Dad came sprinting in to rescue us but because the bottom of the ford was covered in slime, he slipped and went straight on his bum. He got soaked to the skin, I got soaked to the skin, and everybody else ended up absolutely wetting themselves laughing.

For all of us, showing was like one big adventure. During the season we'd be chasing qualifiers for Horse of the Year Show and the Royal International Horse Show up and down the country: Lincolnshire, Cheshire, Devon, Cornwall ... Sometimes, if the show was too far to drive in a day, Mum would bath us kids the evening before, get us in our pyjamas, then put us up in the Luton of our lorry to sleep while Dad drove. We'd wake up the next day at the show and Dad would give us our breakfast and get us dressed in our showing gear while Mum went and got the ponies ready.

Dad liked horses but he didn't love them like Mum did, so while we were competing he'd usually stay in the lorry, chilling out with the motor racing on TV and his special smoked salmon sandwiches. Every now and then he'd nip out to check how we were getting on, then pop back in to catch the end of a race.

My mum always had a bottle of champagne if we did well – for some reason we'd keep the cork and stick a fifty-pence piece in it – and my sister and I would have an ice cream or sweets from one of the vans at the showground. Then we'd get in the lorry and I'd last about five minutes before nodding off, sleep all the way back, and wake up five minutes before we got home to help Mum offload.

I always wanted to win, always. I was a terrible loser and if I made mistakes Mum would be frustrated, I would be frustrated, and then I'd get annoyed and moan like mad. In our kitchen at home we had a big board covered in net with all the rosettes we'd won hooked into it. These were mainly red as we made sure we hid the blue and yellow second- and third-place ones at the bottom because nobody liked looking at those. Emma-Jayne and I didn't compete much against each other because she was older and doing different classes, but we still argued all the time about who'd won what and eventually we had to start writing our names and the date on the back of every single rosette so we had proof.

Because we were on the road so much during the summer, holidays weren't top priority for us. To begin with, we'd go and see my grandfather in Portugal, which was where he moved after divorcing my nan. I hated just lying in the sun, but shopping in the local fruit and veg markets was brilliant – it's something I still love doing now whenever I'm somewhere new – and Mum would also take us for horse and carriage rides as a distraction from being away from the ponies. But as showing began to take up more of our time and money, we were usually too busy to go away and sometimes we ended up missing days at school as well.

It was quite interesting to see how different teachers reacted: Mum would write notes and explain that we were riding at county-level shows, not just mucking around, and some teachers were really nice about it, especially if we won or did well. Some of them didn't give a damn, and a few of them would be cross and make a point of being harder on us.

In my first years at school I found I was quite dyslexic – even the word 'test' made me feel sick to my stomach – and Tuesday spelling lessons with Mrs Watkins at Woodford Primary frightened me to death. (That was another thing I loved about my ponies: as soon as I was on a horse, it was like being granted my freedom. I would start riding and all my worries would just melt away.) Eventually I began to get some extra one-to-one help, and my dad was also great at helping me with my maths because he was so good with figures. Art homework was the one thing I did enjoy because I was such a perfectionist, and I would stay up for hours at night drawing and finishing off, but generally Friday could never come quickly enough throughout my entire time at school.

Spelling tests were one thing; showing was another. I never got nervous before competitions: the bigger the crowd, the more I liked it. Getting to the Royal International Horse Show at Hickstead in July was one of my dreams as a kid. In the morning, classes would be held in the smaller arenas, but if you got through to the championships you'd be in the big main arena with the showjumpers' huge grass Derby bank and everybody watching.

The Horse of the Year Show at Wembley in October was another competition I loved, partly because of the milk float that came round in the morning selling essentials to the people who'd stayed in their lorries overnight. Emma-Jayne and I would worry Dad for money until he gave in and then go and get ourselves milkshakes for breakfast: banana for me and chocolate for Emma-Jayne. Then in the evenings the grown-ups would stay in the lorries and all the kids who'd been competing would go and watch the showjumping in the main arena. We'd have popcorn and ice cream and get told off for talking and being noisy, but as soon as the Whitaker brothers came in everybody would be screaming and shouting the place down, especially if John was on Milton. They were the superstars of my era and had won individual and team golds in the 1989 Europeans, as well as the World Cup Final in 1990 and 1991. One year I can remember seeing Milton in his stable backstage and plucking a few hairs out of his tail because I wanted a souvenir – which I probably shouldn't be admitting.

By the time I was riding at Wembley, I'd gone from lead-rein to first ridden classes with a pony called Cwmtowel Diana. We were quite a successful combination. There was one occasion at a show in Cheshire when we were presented with a trophy by a lady in a green dress, who turned out to be the Queen of Spain.

Diana was really cool but incredibly sharp. My mum had to lunge her for hours before I could get on her, to try and make her as tired as possible, and even then she'd still get quite goey if we were at a show with a lot of atmosphere. I always liked hot horses so it didn't bother me, and Diana was also a really pretty little pony: I used to love competing her because it meant I could wear a pink rose pinned to my jacket to go with her pink diamanté brow band.

Showing was all about that kind of attention to detail, and attention to detail was something Mum was amazing at. She was quite house-proud – we were never allowed posters on our walls, and when she was cleaning at the weekends, she'd kick us all out for the day so we didn't get in her hair. With the ponies, Mum knew all the tricks: dying their tails with Nice'n Easy; chalking their legs to make their socks white; wiping baby oil round their eyes to make them look bigger. If your pony had a black nose you could put a bit of shoe-polish on that as well, but then they'd wipe themselves on you when you tried to lead them in hand and you'd end up with black all down your nice clean shirt sleeves.

The problem was that because image was everything in showing, actually being able to ride didn't matter as much. You'd regularly see kids who didn't know which leg their pony was cantering on, or who didn't know how to turn properly or use the corners of the arena. Often, they'd been plonked on at the last minute: their grooms or their mothers or professional show-pony producers had been the ones riding and training their ponies day in, day out, so when they did find themselves in the ring on what was more-or-less a strange horse, they'd panic and try and get it over with as fast as possible.

At home, Emma-Jayne and I were not only riding under Mum's watchful eye every day, we were also being taught by a friend of hers called Debi Thomas.

Debi had got to know my mum at White Stubbs Farm in the late seventies when Debi was working as an equine nurse. At the time, she was passionate about eventing, but after she got married and had children she decided to switch to dressage and was now aiming to compete at the top level, Grand Prix.

Like my mum, Debi had a fantastic eye for detail, and when she came to teach me and Emma-Jayne she'd make sure we knew how to sit up nice and tall in the saddle and not grip with our legs. She made me think constantly about what I was doing and she always worked me hard, but it paid off.

The showing world was full of cliques and sometimes you'd know who was going to win before you'd even got into the arena. Competitions were judged in two parts and although the first part was all about the pony's conformation, the marks for the second part were awarded for a little individual ridden show. That meant that if a judge wanted a particular horse to win because they knew the owners or the producers, it was quite easy for them to fiddle the results.

That side of it was something I really hated, and the more unfair I thought it was, the more determined I was to win – even then I loved a challenge. One year, I qualified our fourteen-hand hunter pony, Groveside Dexterity (Twiggy), for the Horse of the Year Show at Hickstead. For weeks before I'd been practising my riding with Debi: as part of the show, the judge could sometimes ask you to gallop, and if the grass of the arena was uneven keeping your pony balanced could be hard. But when the judge lined us all up Twiggy and I were way down in thirteenth or fourteenth place out of a class of twenty. It was a boiling hot day and I was wearing my shirt, a waistcoat, a thick tweed jacket and a tie, none of which you were allowed to take off. I had to sit there watching all the other riders do their individual shows, but finally it was my turn and when I'd finished the judge pulled us up to first. Knowing we'd beaten all the professional producers with a horse we'd trained ourselves at home was brilliant, just the best feeling: Mum and I were ecstatic.

As we began to become known as a competing family, people started to send us their ponies to sort out. My parents could only ever afford to buy us difficult ponies anyway so I didn't mind, but there were times when you'd end up on the floor so much you felt like a stunt rider in a rodeo. Mum would pick me up whenever I came off, dust me down, stick me on and send me back for the next round.

That was one of the main differences between my sister and me: you'd have to persuade Emma-Jayne to get back on, whereas I never accepted defeat. It was the same if I had a problem with my riding. I'd be out in the school until I'd fixed it, but if it didn't happen soon for Emma-Jayne, she'd get off, cry and throw her horse in the field. Then I'd get it in from the field, tack it up and sort it out. Obviously, she hated me for it, especially if one of her ponies went better for me than it did for her. We joke about it now but we could be pretty horrible to each other, and my revenge would always be to go off, do something Emma-Jayne couldn't and make sure Mum was watching. 'Mum! Mum! Come and see what I can do!'

One year, my poor sister was unloading her pony, Indie, from the lorry and it stood on her foot and ripped off her toenail. She couldn't ride, and when I took over I ended up qualifying it for Hickstead. That didn't go down very well, nor did the time my mum put me on Buzz, a thirteen-hand dapple-grey hunter pony that was meant to be Emma-Jayne's. For some reason he hated her: it was hard to say what it was about, but they clashed in their ways and generally did not get on. Mum had decided we were going to do some jumping at home one evening and I was fine on my pony, but when Buzz got to the fence he stopped and my sister fell off. She got back on and we went round again, and I jumped the fence and Buzz stopped again and Emma-Jayne went over his head. That was when she got really angry. 'That's it. I've had enough.

I'm going in.' Mum wasn't having any of it. 'Right, Charlotte, you get on.' So I got on Buzz and off we went and jumped the fence.

I felt bad for my sister, especially because Mum used to say that I was the more talented rider. It seems like quite a harsh thing to say, although I think Emma-Jayne realised it was true. I had a natural feel, a sense of what I needed to do when I got on a horse. I think now it must be similar to the way artists work: they have an idea in their mind of what they want to draw, then they get a piece of paper and do it. It's weird, but riding is like that for me. I have a sense in my head of what I want to do, then I get on the horse and somehow I can translate it into the things I do with my legs and seat. My mum always said, 'Charlotte's brains are in her arse.' I like to think it was my natural riding ability she was referring to.

In the early nineties, my dad's business was doing quite well and that was when my parents decided to buy Ardenhall Royal Secret (Millie) for us. Mum had seen Millie in *Horse & Hound* and, although she wasn't for sale, managed to talk her owners into parting with her. Until that point we'd never had expensive ponies, but Millie cost £30,000. She was 12.2 hands and every little girl's dream of a pony: dark liver chestnut with a gloss always on her coat, a white blaze and huge, melting dark eyes. At the time she was being kept in Carmarthenshire at the yard of a producer called Debbie Thomas (another one). The politics of the showing world were such that Mum didn't want to move her, so that meant I had to start going off to Wales at weekends and holidays.

Debbie Thomas's yard wasn't very posh: the stables were converted chicken sheds and the Thomases lived in a mobile home. It was a bit like being away at camp because we slept on mattresses on the floor, but Debbie and her sister Cathy always made you feel looked after. They were both very petite, which meant they could ride kids' ponies themselves, and I never once saw Debbie without a cigarette in her mouth. She'd even smoke when she was riding. The picture I have of her in my head is of someone permanently wearing a riding hat, a pair of chaps and breeches – I don't actually know if she owned any other clothes because while I was there we were all on horses, morning, noon and night.

This was my first real experience of being away from home without my family and during the day it was fine as there were always other kids and their ponies to bundle in with. Night-times were terrible, though. I'd call Mum, crying and begging for her to come and get me. The relief when she came up to see me I can't even begin to describe – to this day, I don't think there's anything that can beat the comfort of a Mum-hug. There were times when I absolutely dreaded having to go, but I would never have refused because I was doing what I genuinely loved.

Kids with tears rolling down their faces was a sight you'd often see at shows, usually because their mothers were screaming at them and/or their ponies were being horrible. Mum was our driver, our groom and our mentor, and she made sure we were one hundred per cent dedicated: we had to be up before school to muck out our ponies, and when we were home we were straight out to do them. But she was never a pushy parent. As far as I was concerned, being in the ring, or in the lorry on the way to a competition with my family round me, was as good as it got.

The best thing about being at Debbie's was that as well as riding Millie, I got to ride all the other ponies that Debbie was producing. The breadth of knowledge and experience it gave me was fantastic, and without it I probably wouldn't be the rider I am today. What I learned is that a horse is like a puzzle with different strengths and weaknesses, and it's your job to put the pieces together and work out how to get the best out of them. Solving that jigsaw is something I still love doing now, and I can honestly say that I find it at least as satisfying as competing.

At Debbie's I was always put on the most awkward ponies in the yard, but the more difficult a pony was, the more I wanted to get on it anyway. There were too many to remember, but Cotspring Song I'll never forget. He was a fourteen-hand hunter pony and when you sat on him he'd rear straight up: the poor girl who was meant to be competing him was petrified.

Horses are clever animals – really clever. If you get on them and you're nervous and tight yourself, they pick up on it straight away. Often I'll see horses being naughty and it's because their rider is scared of them, or not being clear in what they're asking, which is making their horse panicked and stressed. Punishing them is not the answer, and with Cot I knew that the key was staying as calm as possible whenever I rode him.

Gradually we began to develop a bit of a partnership, although my mum never liked watching me on him.

'Charlotte, are you really sure you should be riding that one?'

'Oh, yes, Mum, I'm fine. Really!'

I even qualified him for Hickstead, although I never won on him, which was good as he was the kind of horse who would refuse to go away from other horses: he'd have started doing handstands if you'd asked him to walk out of line to get his prize. Riding Cot, I can

17

say hand on heart, was the only time in my entire career when I've been grateful to come second.

Meanwhile, Millie was justifying my parents' investment and she and my sister were soon going from strength to strength: in 1994 they won eighteen out of eighteen county shows, the Royal International and the Horse of the Year Show. But then things took a horrible turn for the worse.

2

Testing Times

IN OUR FAMILY, Mum stayed at home looking after us kids and Dad was the breadwinner and dealt with the bills. He loved providing for us and giving us things: Molly, my Jack Russell, should have been a goldfish, but Dad was with me when we went to the pet shop and I saw her in her cage. Mum wasn't very pleased with him when we all got home.

'What the hell have you bought now, Ian!'

Dad was always getting into trouble, especially at Christmas. Mum was a real tree artist – still is to this day – but quite careful when it came to money, whereas Dad loved pushing the boat out. For all of us, Christmas was a really special family time. Emma-Jayne and I shared a bedroom but at Christmas my brother would come in with us so we could get up early and muck out the ponies together because none of us was allowed our presents until they'd been done. We'd rush to do them as fast as we could, then we'd go back in and Mum and Dad would make us sing carols outside their bedroom door before we were allowed down to the lounge to see what Santa had left. My parents would put some port and a mince pie out for him, and my dad would spray fake snow round his old wellies so there'd be footprints – honestly, it was ridiculous how convinced I used to be. Food was another big feature of our Christmases, and Dad loved getting the shopping in. 'I'm just going down the road for five minutes,' he'd say, and be gone for two hours.

Probably because he took pride in that role, Dad tried to keep the problems his business was in to himself. That meant the first my mum knew of it was when she got a letter telling her that our house was going to be repossessed.

I was about eight at the time, so too young to understand properly what was going on. What I did know was that we might lose everything, and I saw how upset that made my mum and sister. Mum was crying all the time, and if she saw a van turn in at the top of our lane that she thought might be the bailiffs, she would hide under the table and get my sister to answer the door. What scared me most about it all was that I didn't realise it was just our things they wanted: I thought they'd come to take Mum away.

My parents had different ways of dealing with what was happening to us. Dad was mostly at work and wouldn't really talk about it beyond telling us that it was going to be all right, while Mum was the complete opposite, crying and worrying and stressing. I talked to Emma-Jayne more than I talked to either our mum or dad, and she was the one who explained why we were going to have to go and live somewhere else. Mum says she cried all the way from our old house in Hertfordshire to our new one in Northamptonshire, which I don't remember; what I do remember is Emma-Jayne saying, 'As long as we're still all together, nothing else matters.' I think that comforted Mum a lot and it was what I felt as well, but it must have been awful for Dad. I'm sure Mum kept things from me and I know that our parents' marriage went through a not very good patch after that.

Our new house, The Round House in Holcot, was the first in a long list of rented houses we ended up moving to – we must have changed address six times over the next ten years, depending on how well or badly my dad's business was doing. Each time we went to a new place Mum would stay up all night, putting our things out so it would look like home when we came down in the morning, but I hated the feeling that nothing really belonged to us. Trying to find rented accommodation that would take all the animals was a big worry for Mum too, and when we couldn't afford to rent houses with stables we had to find livery yards for the ponies, which was another cause of stress for her.

Right from the start, Mum told us that there was a chance we would have to sell our ponies. She also told us that she'd do everything she could to keep them and to make sure we could carry on competing. For all of us, including my dad, the ponies were our pride and joy, and having lost so much, I think both our parents wanted to make sure we didn't have to give them up too. That meant there had to be other sacrifices. Millie was probably our greatest asset but my parents wanted to keep her so that I could have the same success on her that Emma-Jayne had had. (Because Emma-Jayne was older she had all our ponies first, then they were handed down to me when she outgrew them.) Millie was also good publicity for Debbie Thomas's yard and Debbie very kindly agreed to pay her running costs so that we could still keep her there. My mum sold her car and my granddad also helped out financially, but it still wasn't enough, so at that point we had to sell our nice horsebox.

Horseboxes are a big deal at competitions, and in the showing world there was so much money that people would often spend up to half a million on an Oakley lorry. They'd be like little houses when you went inside, with showers and toilets and pop-out living areas, so when we started rocking up in our little secondhand lorry, I felt a bit small. But Mum had always taught me it's not what you arrive in, it's what you go home with, and we were still the ones going home with the red rosettes. That was what used to make it feel worthwhile: all the dedication and the making do and the hours we put in. For me, being out there enjoying myself competing was always a release and relief from everything else that was going on, and yes, I'd wish we had a flash lorry or could afford to buy some of the amazing ponies the other kids had, but I tried to turn it round and use it as motivation to make the ponies I did have as good as I could. Looking back now, I think it also made me much more appreciative of things: I remember clearly Mum once telling me that it cost £50 to fill up our lorry with diesel, and it sinking in how much £50 actually was and how hard somebody had had to work to earn it.

The Round House was an old, converted mill. It had six stables and backed almost literally onto the M1. all that stood between you and the road was a field and a big grass embankment, which was meant to cut out some of the noise. Cantering up it was good fitness work for the horses, and it was also where we all went and stood as a family to throw flowers on Princess Diana's funeral cortege as it drove past on 6 September 1997. (I remember the day we found out she'd died because I was made Supreme Champion on Millie at a British Show Pony Society show.)

While we were at The Round House my dad got back on his feet and started a new business, with my mum working for him. I also began following in my sister's footsteps on Millie and together we won both the Royal International and the Horse of the Year Show. But then the inevitable happened and my parents were made an offer for her they couldn't refuse.

Losing Millie was a huge blow for all of us. Even though she was so pretty, she was horrible in the stable: she'd bite and wind-suck and was generally not very nice to handle at all. She'd also managed to nearly knock my front teeth out: I'd fallen off her while I was riding bareback and she tried to jump me and whacked me square on. Mum rushed me to the emergency dentist who sat me in his chair, opened my mouth, said, 'You're not going to like this,' and shoved my teeth back up into my head as hard as he could. 'You'll be all right as long as they don't turn black,' he said before Mum took me home, still trying to wipe the blood off. But for all that, Millie was an amazing little pony when you rode her: she knew her job and she never let you down.

Millie's new owners were Australian. Until then, I hadn't even realised that horses could travel that far, and I was terrified for her in case something happened to her on the flight. Mum did her best to reassure me, but we were all in tears when we said goodbye to Millie. She'd been such a huge part of our lives and given us all so much joy and pleasure and success.

Whenever one of our ponies was sold I cried myself to sleep, although it didn't happen that often because my mum usually couldn't bring herself to do it. But losing rides to other kids was something that I was used to: at Debbie Thomas's I was always qualifying other people's ponies for them to ride at big shows, and had to develop the mentality that it was what it was. My parents rarely kept me in the dark about money, and at the end of the day I realised that if you wanted to keep competing, you had to make sacrifices.

As I got older, I began to compete in more working hunter classes. Working hunters are still judged on their conformation, but you also have to jump a round of rustic fences like the obstacles you might come across out hunting.

When we'd been living at The Round House, one of the things that used to get me through the school day was evenings clear-round showjumping at Norton Heath Equestrian Centre in Blackmore.

Mum would make sure Dylan was ready when I got home and I'd rush back, whip off my school clothes, get all my riding gear on and jump in the lorry. I loved jumping and those evenings were great fun: you paid your £2 and each round the jumps got bigger and bigger, so the longer you stayed there, the higher you could jump.

Dylan had been a little Mountain and Moorland pony, but I now had a proper fourteen-hand working hunter, Enya. I was keen to get better at my jumping, and so Mum arranged for me to have some private lessons with the showjumper Tim Stockdale, who lived nearby.

Tim had first started showjumping for Britain in 1988, and went on to ride at the 2008 Olympics in Beijing. He was also a prospect for London 2012, but then in 2011 he fell off a young horse and fractured his neck in three places. (Luckily he recovered and was back in the saddle four months later.)

Tim was no-nonsense, and a very, very tough coach. I liked tough because I was there to get better and being told what you're doing wrong is the only way you're ever going to improve, but I found Tim's approach quite intimidating. At the age of twelve I wasn't very good at talking to people I didn't know very well, and Tim always wanted you to answer him, even if you didn't know what the answer was. 'Whether it's right or wrong, give me an answer. Never just tell me you don't know.'

I'd get so worried about what I was going to say that I began to freeze and after a bit I started to think I couldn't do anything. Things got better when Laura, Tim's wife, took over and started teaching me instead, but I never felt that I actually wanted to be a showjumper. I was the kind of kid who, if they were given new trainers, kept them in the box for ages, and the showjumpers I saw at competitions always looked far too scruffy for me. My sister and I would be there with our ponies pristine, and they'd have theirs with muck stains on their sides and bits of straw in their tails. It was like a glimpse into another world.

We must have lived at The Round House for four or five years, after which we moved to Woburn in Bedfordshire. My parents managed to find a farmhouse to rent which had a barn with stables, but as there was no arena my sister and I ended up riding in farmers' fields and getting told off for trashing their crops. The farmyard was also used as a base for pheasant shoots in winter, and then there'd be tweedy posh men everywhere, with their socks rolled up to their knees, carrying guns. Unlike me, my brother liked it because he could earn pocket money beating, but it used to be quite a sight when everyone came back with dead birds swinging round their necks.

Moving house meant attending a new school, and at thirteen I started at Vandyke Upper School in Leighton Buzzard. Emma-Jayne was there as well and the funny thing is that we actually got on as long as we weren't at shows competing. If anybody troubled me in class or I came home crying, she'd be very much the big sister and straight on the attack. 'Right, where are they? I'll sort them out.' I take after my mum in that I can be quite blunt and if someone has annoyed me, I'll tell them. But my sister is on a different level and can get really stoked up and a bit scary at times.

Vandyke was where I met my best friend Kayleigh Hawes. There was a big improvement in my homework after I got to know her, mainly because she was the one who was doing it. Kayleigh didn't have her own horse but would do anything to come riding, so the deal ended up being that if she did my homework, she could come over to our house and ride with me. It was great from my point of view, but then I'd get to school and not have a clue what we were doing in class, which was an issue. My teachers would be delighted – 'Oh, Charlotte, you've really improved on this!' – and I'd be sitting there, looking blank.

Both Kayleigh and I thought we'd got the best of the bargain, although sometimes if Kayleigh's mum couldn't drive her and she didn't have money for the bus she'd have to walk to our house, which was a good two miles from hers. At the time it seemed crazy and I couldn't understand why Kayleigh's mum couldn't bring her, but her parents were divorced and her mum was often working. It's only now that I can see how it must have been for Kayleigh back then; because both my parents were always there for me, I never fully realised how lucky I was.

When we weren't with the ponies, or being told off in class for talking about the ponies, or passing notes about the ponies, Kayleigh and I would go off cycling. At weekends we'd cycle to the swimming pool in Woburn, and that was how we'd spend our time while all the other girls started smoking and getting high and rolling their skirts up trying to get boys.

Being teenagers, another thing that was expected of us was that we'd start thinking about our futures, so when we had to choose a work-experience placement I decided I wanted to go to Debi Thomas for a week.

Debi's husband was a stud manager, and when he got a job at Julian Byng's racehorse stud at Wrotham Park in Hertfordshire, the Thomases moved to a bungalow in the grounds. Wrotham Park is a neo-Palladian country house set in 300 acres, and after we'd moved to a house without an arena, my mum would take me there for lessons with Debi. It was a bit like going into a fairytale, although being a kid I didn't really appreciate it at the time: you rode down from the stables through a beautiful wood to a school that was completely surrounded by trees.

Debi had her own livery business at Wrotham Park, but she was still competing in dressage and every time I'd see her she'd tell me I was wasted on show ponies and should be doing dressage instead. I usually ignored her because it wasn't something that inspired me: showing was what I was successful at and what all my friends did, so I didn't see any reason to change. But one day while I was on work experience Debi suddenly decided she was going to put me on Truday, the horse she was training up to Grand Prix.

I always leaped at the chance to ride anything new, although when Debi brought Truday out of her stable I did a double take. She seemed absolutely massive for one thing, at least 16.2, and although she had a really pretty face she'd have been terrible for showing because she had a roach back, which meant that her bum was slightly higher than her withers.

Show horses have to be absolutely perfect with not a lump or bump on them anywhere, so it was news to me that dressage horses could come in all shapes and sizes – fat, thin, long, short. Then I had another shock when I saw Truday's saddle: showing saddles are small and petite and neat, whereas dressage saddles are like big squares with deep seats and thick knee rolls. How was I meant to sit in that?

It felt completely different to everything I'd been used to, but we hacked down through the trees as usual and

Debi got me to warm Truday up. Then, out of nowhere, she told me to do a flying change. Well, I had no idea what one of those was.

A flying change is when a horse skips from leading with one leg to the other while it's cantering, but I couldn't follow Debi's explanation at all and just sat there, nodding away, totally lost. Even as she sent me off cantering around the arena I still had no clue what I was doing, but then I put my leg back behind the girth like I'd been told and to my complete surprise I felt Truday skip and start leading with her other leg. We did it a couple more times, then Debi told me to try some fours (changing legs every four strides), and after that a half-pass.

By now I was so out of my comfort zone: all my ponies ever had to do was walk, trot, canter and go in a straight line, and suddenly here I was on a great big dressage horse doing tricks. The tempi changes I found quite hard because of the timing, but when I asked Truday for the half-pass she didn't hesitate – I was going sideways across the arena before I even knew it. It was amazing: all I could think was, 'Wow! This is *so cool*!'

As strange as it was for me, Truday didn't bat an eyelid: it was just a normal day's schooling for her. What was harder – and what she would need to perfect if she was going to be a Grand Prix horse – was piaffe/passage.

Piaffe is basically trotting on the spot, and passage is like piaffe but your horse creeps forward instead of staying still: it's slower and much more springy than normal trot. It turned out that to improve Truday's piaffe, she needed someone on her back while Debi worked her from the ground, which was where I came in.

My job was to make little half-halts with my reins to stop Truday moving forward while Debi tapped a lunge whip lightly on her hind legs. Almost at once Truday began to piaffe. I don't think either of us could believe it.

Piaffe was fun, but when I tried passage, that turned out to be even more fun: Truday was not only getting the elevation and lift off the ground, she was also moving forward so it really did feel like we were dancing. I think the whole time we were doing it I must have been grinning from ear to ear, because my entire face was aching by the time Mum took me home.

Truday and Debi were the first pieces to fall into place; the next piece was Charlie McGee.

He was a fifteen-hand Irish thoroughbred bought by my parents as a working hunter from a producer called Rory Gilsenan. When we left Woburn and moved to another new house, this time without stables, Rory took our ponies as liveries at his yard in Fringford. I stopped keeping track of our houses after that because if the ponies weren't at home it didn't matter to me where we lived, but having them with Rory was great.

Being a certain type of Irishman, Rory's every other word was 'See you next Tuesday'; he also used to terrorise me by making me jump anything that crossed our paths. We'd be out hacking together and he'd start eyeing up massive great hedges or five-bar gates. 'Go on, Charlotte. Just kick on down there! Go on, kick on down! You'll be fine!' I was totally fearless so would do whatever he said, and he was always sticking me on anything he had in his yard, which I loved. The only downside was that you had to be a bit patient: often I'd be doing my ponies while Rory's grooms were getting his horses ready, and we'd all be finished and tacked up and ready to go and Rory was still nowhere to be seen. I'd call up to the house, and Rory would call back that he'd be there in a minute, and five minutes later I'd still be standing waiting. Eventually I'd have to go up to the house myself, and at that point I'd discover he was either asleep or sitting in the kitchen with his feet up, fag in one hand and mug of coffee in the other. I was forever having to go and root him out, but he was great fun, if a bit crazy: one day when he was creosoting his fences he decided he was going to paint me as well and so we ended up having a full-on creosote fight.

When we first bought Charlie from Rory he was only four years old. At the time he didn't look anything special – a bit scrawny with no neck – but he had the cutest, cheeky face and he was brave, too: with Rory constantly telling you to 'Kick on down, there!' you soon found out you could jump higher than you thought you could.

After getting the feel of piaffe on Truday I knew what I was aiming for, so one day I thought to myself, 'I'm going to teach Charlie McGee to do that.' I found a big field while we were out hacking and started playing around, but it seemed like no matter what I did, it wasn't happening: Charlie was a show horse and had no idea what I wanted him to do. I knew then that I somehow had to find a way of learning more, so the next time Mum and I were in RB Equestrian in Milton Keynes I decided I'd get a DVD and try and teach myself. And that was how Carl Hester first entered my life, because it was his DVD that I ended up buying.

At the time I barely knew the name Carl Hester and I certainly didn't know how good he was. Carl had grown up on Sark, which famously has no cars, riding a donkey called Jacko. From those beginnings he'd gone on to compete for Britain at the 1990 World Championships and 1991 European Championships, and he'd also been the youngest-ever British rider to compete at an Olympics when he rode at Barcelona in

1992. Carl himself had been trained by the legendary Dr Bechtolsheimer in Germany, so if you were going to try and learn dressage from a DVD, you'd at least want it to be one of Carl's.

I can remember now watching this DVD while lying on the floor of our lounge, completely mesmerised. When Carl explained how he was going to introduce suspension into his horse's trot it looked so easy: 'I pick up my reins, I half-halt the front, I click with my voice and touch with my leg, and this is the reaction.' I can still hear him saying it. But of course Carl was a top international rider riding a top dressage horse, and poor Charlie was a thoroughbred show pony so built completely differently. His natural movement was small and tense and tight through his shoulders, and when I first tried to get the elevation and suspension from him he didn't move an inch. But I kept on persevering and when he did finally get it I was so proud of myself. Mum had thought I was just being a crazy child again when I told her what I was planning to do, but when she saw me and Charlie passaging away round the field, she absolutely loved it.

By now, Emma-Jayne had given up showing: she'd won everything she could as a child, and since she'd left school she'd decided to go into producing ponies as a career. She was really good at it, too: if you wanted to make your horse look a million dollars, you'd want Emma-Jayne.

But I was also getting to the age where I had to decide about the future, and although I'd always thought I'd carry on with showing as an adult, now it was coming down to it, I realised I'd actually lost my passion for it.

Part of the reason was Hez: like Charlie, he was a fifteen-hand, bright bay working hunter and when my parents bought him he was only five, so quite green and spooky. I absolutely loved him, but one day we found him down in the stable, rolling with colic. The vet operated, but the twist in his gut was too bad and Hez had to be put to sleep. I'd never lost a horse before like that and it was horrible, not something you'd want anyone to go through.

Losing Hez was a turning point because I realised that I didn't want to go off, get another new pony and carry on with that. But even before Hez the shine had gone off the showing world for me. Your pony's way of going often wasn't taken into consideration, and with the irregularities in the judging I was starting to wonder why I bothered: you'd travel all round the country and ride well only to lose out to people who really didn't deserve to win. Added to that, in showing, the ridden element was marked as a whole out of twenty; in dressage, every single move was marked out of ten. To be really good at it you couldn't just do one thing well, you needed to teach your horse to do every movement well, which really appealed to my perfectionist side.

The final piece to fall into place was Ian Cast. He has been with me on every step of my journey, so he's worth introducing properly.

Ian was born in Essex in 1977 into a completely non-horsey family. Then, when Ian was twelve, he and his brother were taken to the beach where they had a donkey ride. Ian's brother hated it, but Ian was hooked. After he left school, Ian studied for a National Diploma in Equine Science at Writtle College in Chelmsford and went on to get his British Horse Society (BHS) exams up to Assistant Instructor level. For a time he had worked at a dressage-based riding school in Kent, but he had then moved to Buckinghamshire to work at the yard of the international dressage rider Judy Harvey, who was based near Milton Keynes.

The first time I met Ian was at a livery yard in Drayton Parslow: my parents had recently moved again, this time to a house behind Addington Manor Equestrian Centre, which had meant the ponies needed a new home, too. I was spending weekends at the yard mucking out, riding my horses and earning money by helping other people with theirs, and that was how I happened to see Ian giving lessons to two sisters. I liked the way he taught and he seemed warm and friendly, so I asked him if he'd have time to teach me as well.

We clicked instantly – I don't know what it was, but Ian to me felt like the big brother I'd never had. Over the years he's been at my side literally every step of the way, and to this day I rely on him both as the most loyal friend you could ever wish for and as an extra pair of eyes on the ground. He's one of the few people I can stand having around me before a show and has been there for me at all of the big occasions.

As an instructor, Ian was great: constructive and always giving me lots of ideas and exercises to work on. He had a good laugh when I told him I'd watched a DVD of Carl and taught my Charlie to do a 'big trot' – at the time I didn't really know how to describe what I was doing – but when he saw what I'd actually managed, I think he was quite amazed.

I've never asked Mum whether we ended up in Addington by accident or not, because although Addington Manor was quite new at the time, it would soon become one of the top training venues in the country. Dressage competitions were held there all the time, and after I'd been having lessons with Ian for a month or two, Mum thought Charlie and I were ready to give one a go.

I began at the bottom, preliminary, which was very simple: walk, trot, canter and some circles. There were no top hats and tails – I just went along in my showing gear. But unlike showing, I had to learn a set test, whereas before I had been used to a judge simply telling me what they wanted me to do on the day.

That was a big change for me, and the other difference I really noticed was how quick it all was.

In showing you might have twenty ponies in a class, which meant that you could be sitting in an arena for hours waiting for everybody to have their turn. Then once everyone had ridden you'd have to dismount and unsaddle your pony so that the judges could look at its conformation, saddle up, get back on again and stand waiting in line while they made up their minds about marks. If it was torrential rain, you sat in it. If it was boiling hot, you sat in it. It used to be never-ending: you'd start chatting to the kid next to you because you were so bored and by the time it was over and you came out of the ring you'd know their entire life story. My first dressage test was done and dusted in four and a half minutes, and all I could think was, 'Is that it? We can go home?' It turned out we could: we got our mark, found out who'd won, finished.

I seem to remember I scored 58 per cent for that first test and I genuinely didn't know if that was good or bad, it was all so new to me. When Mum and I got back to the lorry, I excitedly rang Debi Thomas to tell her. 'That's a good start, Charlotte,' she said, 'but obviously there are some things to work on.'

Little did either of us know I'd one day be scoring over 90 per cent.

3

Earning My Spurs

I LEFT SCHOOL at sixteen with ten GCSEs, including a few Cs and a B in art. Looking back I almost wish I'd done a bit better because I can see now what a small part of life it takes up, but at the time I just could not wait to get out of the place.

Now that I'd decided to focus on dressage and didn't have school getting in the way, I could spend my days with Charlie at Drayton Parslow. I looked after him and had lessons with Ian, and the rest of my time I was mucking out, getting horses in and out from the field, doing clipping jobs and anything else that would earn a bit of money.

Even with what I'd taught him, Charlie was still a show pony and never going to be good enough to be a proper dressage horse. The problem was that dressage horses were expensive, and I knew my parents couldn't afford to buy one – which was why, when we did get one, it was mostly by accident.

Twice a year a centre in Buckinghamshire staged an equine sale, and Mum and I would always go along because we lived so near. On the day that Renegade came up we both noticed him, at first because he was so stunning, and then again because he didn't sell.

René's dad was Gribaldi, a black Trakehner stallion and famous dressage sire. René was also black and had a white star and four crystal-white socks, so when you saw him it was a bit like Black Beauty come to life. He

35

was black and beautiful and cheap, and I can honestly say those were the reasons we ended up getting him. Mum and I never planned or discussed it, and we didn't really have any idea what we were buying – as we soon realised.

The woman who owned René was called Sandra Biddlecombe. Sandra would end up being a big part of my life and it seems funny now to think it was René who introduced us because it was probably the only good thing he ever did. He may have been amazing to look at, but he was a pig to ride. He was awkward and lazy and on the ground he'd drag me everywhere – he put me off black horses forever. We got him as a three-year-old and when we sold him a couple of years later there was not a single tear shed: he was the only horse I've ever had who I've waved merrily on his way.

With Charlie, I now had two horses I could compete, but even though I was still learning from Ian we both knew I needed to take the next step up. Ian's boss, Judy Harvey, sometimes took working pupils, so one day Ian suggested I get in touch with her and see if she'd give me some lessons or even consider taking me on.

Judy Harvey was (and is) an international rider, judge, trainer and commentator. She had run a riding school in London for ten years, then an equestrian centre in Stow-on-the-Wold, and by 2002 was managing the yard of a man called Richard Heley, who was in corporate finance but also had an interest in dressage.

When I sat on my bed to ring her I was absolutely petrified because I still wasn't great at talking to new people and I'd heard Judy was quite scary. But she told me to come to the yard to meet her and it must have gone OK because by the end of it she'd agreed to take me on as a working pupil.

Over the course of my career I've often competed against and worked with Judy and she's someone I feel genuinely lucky to know. But let me tell you, I'm still scared of that lady to this day: imagine Meryl Streep in *The Devil Wears Prada*.

Riding was a privilege you had to earn at Judy's: first you had to put in the graft. That meant doing all the hard, dirty jobs – mucking out, washing windows, cleaning tack – 8 a.m. until 5.30 p.m., six days a week. It wasn't a big yard, just two small barns opposite Richard's house, but keeping it tidy was a nightmare. It always had to be swept spotlessly clean, and all the cobwebs in the barns had to come down, which was a job I hated doing.

Good stable management was everything at Judy's yard – it was all very strict and British Horse Society. At home, for example, we'd never tie up the horses when we were mucking out, we'd just drag the wheelbarrow into the stable. Obviously it was dangerous because your horse could get its legs caught up, but until I went to Judy's I'd never been taught things like that. In her eyes, learning to take care of your horse properly was just as important as being able to ride it well, so we'd have lessons on how to fit tack, how to bandage your horse's legs, how to take their temperatures, how to brush them properly – everything. Then sometimes you'd finish your day and she'd suddenly decide to do a snap inspection: all the horses' rugs had to be taken off and if there was even the tiniest mark or trace of sweat you'd know all about it.

'That's not good enough! People are paying money to have their horses here. Do it again!'

It was a great way to learn because you never made the same mistake twice.

One of the nice things about being at Judy's was that I knew Ian would be there. On days when Judy had shouted me out, I knew at least I could talk to him and tell him what I'd done wrong. He'd always tell me not to worry and to keep going and then he'd come out with the Hobnobs – he was addicted to Hobnobs at that point.

I also got to know Roland Tong, who was another working pupil and who would later ride for Ireland at the 2013 Europeans and the 2014 World Equestrian Games. Roland was very, very competitive, and as I was very, very competitive as well, if we ended up competing against each other then it was war. Roland was a very serious person and before shows he used to get through packs of cigarettes because he was so nervous. You didn't want to be around him when it didn't go to plan, but generally we'd bounce off each other, and because he was older and more experienced he would often help me.

Next to Ian, however, the person I spent most time with was Jayne Turney. If Ian was like a brother to me, Jayne was like a sister.

She was another working pupil and lived on-site. She'd brought with her a little sixteen-hand coloured mare who was really pretty but had such an attitude no one else but Jayne could ride her. Watching them together was just hilarious. Jayne was really mellow and calm and never in a bad mood; her horse was feisty, feisty, feisty. If Jayne asked her to do something she didn't want to, she'd give a cow-kick with her hind legs. She could be a little witch and you could just imagine her as a human, giving you the finger and telling you to eff off, but Jayne being the way she was, they seemed to suit each other and even each other out.

Because I was still living at home just down the road, Ian, Roland and Jayne often ended up coming back for dinner. Mum loved having people round and is a great cook, but honestly, I have never seen anybody eat like Jayne. Mum used to pile a mountain of food on her plate and she'd eat the whole lot, then if anybody had any leftovers, she'd clear those as well. I don't know where she put it, because she's the slimmest person and never gained any weight.

Ian and Jayne were like part of the family and so it wasn't really a surprise when they ended up moving in. Ian, who is gay, stayed for a few months after he broke up with his boyfriend and needed to find a new place to rent, but Jayne was with us for several years and went into business producing ponies with my sister when she left Judy's.

After a couple of months I was allowed to bring René to Judy's, which was a perk of being a working pupil. He was as new to dressage as I was, though, so Judy often taught me on Richard Heley's schoolmaster, Wow Voyager (Wiz).

Wiz was German-bred and a true gentleman, but he was also 17.2 hands. If I'd just come off Charlie, that was a lot of horse. He also had the bounciest trot imaginable, and I think of all the things I learned at Judy's, learning to sit to that trot was the hardest.

The more I tried to keep still, the more I bounced everywhere. Judy would be shouting, 'Relax! Let your hips go with the motion!' and I'd be jiggling almost out of the saddle. It was like trying to sit on top of a washing machine: you'd never want to have breakfast before you tried it.

It was only when Judy put me on the lunge and took my stirrups away that I began to get the hang of it and could let the weight sink down into my heels. We realised when I got them back that part of the problem was I'd been trying to ride with them too short, which was another old habit: in showing, being able to use your legs effectively mattered less than the picture they created on the saddle.

I don't regret any of the experience I got from showing. I realise it might sound as though I'm a bit down on it now, but that absolutely isn't the case. Showing taught me ringcraft, it taught me how to perform in front of big crowds from a young age, it made me take pride in myself and my pony, and it also meant that I'd been used to riding in a double bridle from a young age. But when I got to Judy's, it did begin to sink in how much ground I had to make up.

Faced with this, Jayne and I decided that we were going to up our game together. Because I was having such problems with sitting trot we started off by going swimming to develop our core strength, which is essential given that you're having to absorb the whole movement of your horse through your own body. A lot of riders rely on their reins to hang on and balance, because unless you're fit you can't support yourself independently. Obviously, it's much nicer for your horse if you're strong enough not to have to hang on to his back teeth all the time, although even now, when I regularly ride nine hours a day, my stomach muscles will start to burn if I'm doing sitting trot on a horse I'm not used to.

Jayne and I would get up early and go to the gym before we started work, do our fifty or seventy lengths, then at lunchtimes or in the evenings we'd sit down and watch DVDs of the riders we admired.

The one we ended up studying most was of the 2005 World Cup Finals in Las Vegas, which was won by Anky van Grunsven of the Netherlands. Edward Gal was second on Lingh (also for the Netherlands) and the American rider Debbie McDonald was third.

At that point, Anky was the queen of dressage – in 2006, she would be the first rider ever to score over 80 per cent – but Debbie was in front of a home crowd. When she got to her final centre line and passaged all the way down it to Aretha Franklin's 'Respect', every single one of the 11,500 people in that crowd were on their feet. They were all rooting for her and stamping and clapping their hands the whole way, but neither Debbie nor Brentina, her mare, lost focus one bit: it was jaw-dropping – complete OMG stuff.

The other rider I loved to watch was Germany's Isabell Werth, who is one of my heroes to this day. The rivalry between the Germans and the Dutch was the big story when I was growing up, and Isabell and Anky's battle dominated dressage for years. Isabell was ridiculously talented and although her horse, Gigolo, perhaps wasn't as expressive as Anky's Bonfire, she could always pull out the best in whatever she rode.

In many ways, Isabell was one of the riders who made me: there seemed to be nothing that would stop her. She doesn't always have the most spectacular horses but she is a genius rider and her training is incredible. I always found watching her quite funny because if she made a mistake she'd start muttering away to herself all around the arena, but when she did something well she'd pat her horse and smile and look like she was having the most jolly time.

I liked that she could show she was pleased, but would never let a hiccup or two throw her off course: she'd grit her teeth and carry on riding and fighting until the bitter end. It was an attitude I learned a lot from. Sometimes you've just got to pull it together, get on with it, and forget whatever else might have happened.

When I started at Judy's in November 2002 I was on £40 a week. Living at home I didn't need to pay rent, and because I was a working pupil René's livery was free. But there was still Charlie to pay for, so everything

41

I had was going back to Mum for his upkeep, and as £40 doesn't go very far I was always trying to earn more.

One of the first jobs I found was as a pot-washer at a local pub. It ended up being for one night only. I don't quit easily but I was stuck out in a tiny kitchen the entire time and by the end of it my back was killing me, my hands were all shrivelled up, and I can honestly say I'd rather have gone and mucked out more stables for a few extra pounds than spent another second doing that.

My next job was clipping horses for a local dealer called Mr Prater who bought and sold showjumpers. Because he'd always have people coming to look at them they had to be immaculate, not a line of hair left anywhere, and they also had to be fully clipped: heads, bodies, legs – the whole shebang. I was working with Mr Prater's son Daniel, and together we'd do seven or eight horses a day. We'd divide it up between us – Daniel would do the legs and I'd do the body and heads – and if the horse was quiet we could get it done in an hour. If it was difficult or misbehaving the vet would have to sedate it, which would make it sweat, and if a horse is sweating too much you can't get the hair off. It was back-breaking, horrible work and you'd itch all day long because the hair would get everywhere – up your nose, down your clothes, in your bra – but it earned me money, so I did it. (And it taught me to clip really well.)

Hard work was constant, but there were also some fun times off.

I'd never been the type of person who was interested in going out at weekends with my friends and getting completely hammered, although my sister sometimes tried to get me into nightclubs underage with fake ID (as you do). It never appealed: sometimes, girls at the yard would turn up on a Monday morning looking absolutely knackered, and that would really put me off because I never wanted to be in a position where I couldn't do my job properly and get Judy angry with me. But then one night I somehow got dragged into going to Pink Punters, one of Milton Keynes's gay clubs, with Ian and a group of his friends.

We got a taxi from the yard, which was where things started to go wrong because while we were waiting someone produced a bottle of champagne. I must have had a couple of glasses, but because I never drank it got me completely wasted to the point where I couldn't even stand up. The others managed to get me to the club, but as soon as I was there I collapsed on a settee. Luckily, a friend of mine, Martin, was in that night and took pity on me when I started begging him to get me home. 'I can't take you home,' he said, 'but I can get you to the White Hart.' This was a pub near our house and by then anywhere that wasn't that club was good enough for me. So Martin got me into his car and while he was driving he called my brother to come and collect me. Unfortunately, by the time Charles arrived at the White Hart I'd got my second wind and thought I quite wanted to stay there and drink some more.

My loving brother was absolutely furious. He never really drank much either, and he knew how out of character being drunk was for me. I was still insisting on staying, so without further ado he picked me up, threw me over his shoulder and literally carried me out, with me hitting him on the bum and yelling, 'Put me down! I don't want to go! Put me down!' all the way.

Ian was responsible for another unforgettable night when he took me to G-A-Y in London. I was still pretty innocent at this point, even after the night out at Pink Punters, so this was literally the biggest eye-opener of my entire life. Not only were there guys doing all sorts in the toilets, there were also hes dressed as shes, which left me completely gobsmacked.

Ian loves his music and had even once auditioned for *Pop Idol*, so he was delighted to see Holly Valance performing her old hit, 'Kiss Kiss'. But then when we finally left at 2.00 a.m. there were no taxis to be seen. There was only one option: we were going to have to walk all the way back across London to where we were staying at Ian's brother's. Unusually for me I had high heels on, and after a bit the balls of my feet were so sore I couldn't walk another step. The only way I was going to make it back was to take them off, and so that's how I ended up walking the streets of London at night, barefoot. It was absolutely disgusting: there was dirt and glass and people peeing up walls wherever you looked. I have to say it was probably one of the worst nights of my life: never, never, never again.

* * *

Because Mum had followed Debi's dressage career and also watched me ride Truday, she was completely supportive of my new path. While I was at Judy's she'd come and watch me have lessons, and because she'd ridden so much herself it was always useful to have another pair of eyes on me. I think it was a learning experience for her, too – most of the time.

Judy would sometimes have lessons from the Dutch trainer Bert Rutten, and if I was lucky Bert would give me some time as well. He was the son of an Olympic dressage rider and had ridden at several European and World Championships in the eighties. He'd trained many horses to Grand Prix and so his rates were quite expensive, but if you got more than six or seven words from him in an hour you were doing well.

Bert was very tall and while he watched you he'd sit at the side of the arena, long legs crossed, with a little farmer's hat on his head and smoking a cigar. If you did something well, he'd say, 'Good, good,' thoughtfully, and if you did something that wasn't good, he'd just sit there and say nothing.

It doesn't sound particularly helpful, but the few things he did actually say really made sense and could make a huge difference. I think my mum was a bit baffled, though, because I'd come out of the arena and she'd often say, 'Well, what did you get out of that?'

Part of the reason why Judy got on so well with Bert was because they were both big believers in self-reliance. 'I'm here to help you, but not for you to rely on,' Judy would say, which I thought was very, very clever. It always stuck in my head that I needed to feel for myself if what my horse was doing was right or wrong, not rely on someone to tell me. All dressage riders and trainers use earpieces so that they can communicate with each other easily even if they're in a crowded warm-up arena, but riders sometimes fall apart when they have to take their earpiece out. Ultimately, you're on your own when you're out there competing, and Judy believed that from day one you should be learning to stand on your own two feet. She was absolutely right, but it was a very hard lesson for me to learn.

The first time I competed on Wiz was at a Premier League competition at Addington and it almost didn't happen. The night before as I was finishing work, Judy came over to check on me and make sure everything was OK.

'Oh, yes, Mum's coming down to plait Wiz in the morning and ...'

'No, she's not. You're doing it. You're old enough now.'

'But I can't plait!'

'Well, you'd better learn.'

This was at six o'clock in the evening. In a complete panic, I phoned home. 'Mum! Mum! You have to come and teach me how to plait! Judy says that unless I do it, I'm not allowed to go to the show tomorrow!'

It wasn't out of laziness that I hadn't learned, but I probably had got into the habit of Mum doing things for me. When we went to a show she would drive the lorry, plait up and make the ponies look pretty, and I'd get myself ready, get on and ride: that was my part of the job. Then after we'd finished, Mum would untack the pony, wash it off, put it away and drive home. I look back now and think that if I'd been the adult, I probably would have wanted my child to be more independent at a younger age, but Mum loved it and it was what all the showing mums did.

To plait a horse's mane you first have to divide the hair into equal sections. If your horse has a long neck, the sections are bigger so there are fewer plaits and its neck looks shorter; if your horse has a short neck, it's the other way round. You damp the hair down, divide it up, do your plait, roll it up and then stitch it round with a needle and thread so it's secure. This was what Mum had to teach me all in the space of a few hours and by the time we'd finished it was nearly dark. They weren't brilliant plaits – definitely not like Mum's – but they were good enough and didn't come out when Wiz shook his head. We also ended up winning our class the next day, so it turned out pretty well, although at the time it all felt like a lot to take in.

* * *

July 2003 brought my eighteenth birthday. At the time I loved pavlova, so Judy and Malcolm, her husband, threw a party for me complete with a huge pavlova made by their friend and house guest, Tjaart Walraven. Nowadays, Tjaart is the Paul Hollywood of *The Great South African Bake Off*, and even then he was an amazing cook. He was also a real character, and because he was bubbly and his sense of humour was like mine it could be a nightmare between the two of us. He was always trying to get me to stop working so I would go off and have fun with him, and one day when he thought I was being boring he decided he was just going to cover me in Fairy Liquid and tip a bucket of water on me. Obviously, I frothed up all over the place. I chased him down the drive, yelling at him, and then we both got in trouble with Judy for mucking about.

I think she was hoping we'd get together, and one evening she and Malcolm and Tjaart and I were invited for dinner at the home of Stephen Clarke, a former international rider and now a very senior FEI (International Equestrian Federation) judge. Tjaart could play the piano and as I'd had a few lessons from a neighbour as a kid, we ended the evening playing a duet together ... but that was as far as it went.

Or, as far as it went with Tjaart. At around the same time, I'd started going out with another of Judy's working pupils, Chris. He was a very good rider, but his parents, who lived up north, were quite tricky. His father was a builder and his mother thought neither of us would ever really succeed in our careers because we didn't have the money she thought dressage required. They made it pretty difficult for us, and although we were together for a couple of years, Chris eventually got pushed into giving up and going back home to work with his dad. The hardest part for me was that Chris didn't really say anything, he just left. That got me more than anything. It was obviously over as far as he was concerned, but I was heartbroken for a while.

Trying to get my own career off the ground was a struggle, definitely. Wow Voyager was great but very much Richard's, and Richard had his fixed riding days and I had mine. Sometimes he would generously agree to swap, but I often couldn't ride as much as I needed to before a show, and trying to compete on a horse that I couldn't train properly was difficult.

By now we'd sold Charlie McGee: René was the horse I needed to concentrate on for the future, and we couldn't afford to keep them both. It was sad to see Charlie go, but we sold him to Debi Thomas for her daughter to ride, so I knew he was going to have a home for life.

Unfortunately time wasn't improving things between René and me – I've still got the scar on my arm from when he towed me off one day. We were just about to go to a show and I'd chalked all his socks so they were crystal white and he looked a picture. Then I went to lead him up the ramp of the horsebox and he thought, 'No, thanks,' and shot off in full, flat-out gallop up Judy's drive. I wasn't going to let go because I'd got him all groomed and plaited and ready, but he tore my breeches, ripped my arm open and then, just to add insult to injury, went straight for a ploughed field. I was absolutely furious. I had to get him back to the yard, spray all the mud off his legs, get him in the lorry, get changed and still make it to the show and ride. I can't even remember how I did it, but I was pretty stressed, as you can imagine.

The two of us were never meant to be, but we weren't really looking for a replacement because of the expense. Then Mum saw Fernandez.

* * *

In 2002 my nan had died, leaving my mum quite a big inheritance. After the money came through, she was able to put down a deposit, which meant that she and my dad could finally raise a mortgage and have a home of their own again. The rest of the money she set aside for a rainy day, but that ended up arriving sooner than she expected.

Fernandez, like René, wasn't a horse Mum set out to buy. She knew what I liked, though, and when she saw him treating people like crash-test dummies, she thought, 'That's the perfect horse for Charlotte.'

Because I was working I didn't see Dez myself until the moment the auction began. It was an evening event, my sister had come with us, and as the bidding started to go higher and higher we were all getting more and more nervous. Every time the price went up by £1,000, my sister would start elbowing Mum in the ribs. 'Go on, Mum! Go on!' Meanwhile, I sat on the other side of her, desperately trying to stop her putting her hand up. 'No, Mum! It's too much! No! No more!'

My sister had turned into my biggest supporter as we'd both grown up; she was also still full-on about everything, including spending Mum's inheritance money for her. I wanted Fernandez just as badly, not least because Judy had also been to look at him and given him her seal of approval, but I was horrified that so much money was being spent on getting him for me.

Mum kept putting her hand up and my sister kept egging her on, and then Mum put her hand up one more time and, just like that, the bidding stopped and the hammer went down. What neither Mum nor I knew was that Fernandez no longer had a reserve. Mum had been happily bidding away, thinking she was safe up to

£20,000, which was where the reserve had been set. But nobody had thought to tell us that it had been taken off, so when on the night the hammer came down at £18,000, that was it – Dez was ours.

None of us knew whether to be in total shock or leaping out of our seats. I hadn't even met my new horse yet, and when we went round the back of the indoor school to see him he was tiny, no more than 15.3 hands. I think even Mum was taken aback. He'd looked big when he was ridden because he had such presence and the air of a real showman; he was also built well, with his neck set in such a way that he naturally looked very uphill. But up close I really didn't think he was going to be big enough. 'Well, he's three, so he's still growing,' Mum said, I think trying to put a brave face on it.

Dez was a Westphalian gelding by the champion stallion Florestan. He was a real red chestnut with two white socks and a white blaze and he had the biggest, loveliest eyes. When I go to buy a horse now I'll always look in their eyes because it will often tell you a lot about their character: 90 per cent of the time if you see a kind eye, you've got a kind horse. Apart from sometimes bolting, that was Dez all over: he had a lovely nature, loved affection and attention, and would get you to spend hours cuddling and scratching him.

Unfortunately, because he was so young and not yet used to being ridden, he also had sores all round his mouth from the bit, and there were sores where the girth and bridle had gone. You felt so sad looking at him, and Judy told us that the best thing we could do would be to let him forget the whole experience of the auction, turn him out in the field, and not touch him for four months.

It was winter when we got Dez and the fields were absolutely filthy, ankle-deep in mud. As he'd been clipped, I thought I'd at least go and get him some nice warm rugs and neck covers to go to sleep in so he didn't feel cold, and each morning and evening I'd stop on the way to Judy's to give him some feed and a carrot or apple. I'd call his name from the gate and he'd prick his ears up and come cantering over to see me as soon as he heard my voice. It was so nice seeing him grow up and get stronger in front of my eyes because it was obviously what he needed – but at the same time, not being able to get on him straight away was pretty hard.

4

On the Right Pathway

By EARLY 2004 I'd made it to Advanced Medium level on Wow Voyager, which meant getting to grips with half-passes, walk pirouettes and the odd flying change. We were also competing in Young Rider classes, where top hats and tailcoats were compulsory. Getting mine felt like the ultimate goal, and putting them on I felt so proud, although I did think I had to then go out and deliver the goods: I didn't want to be all the gear and no idea.

I'd been involved with the British Young Riders Dressage Scheme, BYRDS, and Dressage UK Under 21s for several years by this point. The latter was run by Carol Hogg and at one of my first events, a talent-spotting day at Addington in October 2002, I came sixth out of six on Charlie McGee. Fortunately, I managed to redeem myself at another event, a ride-off where we all swapped horses. I don't remember anything about the one I was riding, but I do know I got 78 per cent. BYRDS, which was the British Dressage-affiliated version of Carol's organisation, had been set up in 1990 by the dressage rider Dane Rawlins and the financier Egon von Greyerz, whose daughter was then on the Young Riders European team. The idea of BYRDS was to bring young riders together and develop a bit of team spirit, and also to get different trainers and speakers to share their expertise through lectures and events.

By the time I got involved with it, Dane was running BYRDs with Jennie Loriston-Clarke, who was pretty much equestrian royalty. Jennie's brother Michael and sister Jane had both ridden at the Olympics, her sister Sarah had been in the film *International Velvet*, her mother had founded the Catherston Stud in Hampshire, and Jennie herself had ridden at the Olympics four times.

The first time I remember seeing Jennie was at a long-reining demonstration with her Olympic horse Dutch Gold: I just could not believe that Jennie wasn't even on his back and she was still getting him to do piaffe and passage. Then they went into canter and started doing one-time changes, which really did blow my mind: Jennie had the reins going like skipping ropes, and Dutch Gold was just swinging along, skipping from side to side between them.

Jennie was one of the most brilliant riders and trainers I'd ever seen. She obviously had an incredible gift for working with horses, so my monthly lessons with her used to make me pretty nervous. I was so new to it all and always wondered what she was going to think of what I was doing, but Jennie never made me feel intimidated and would get really stuck in with me.

The chance to pick up different techniques and work with different trainers was something I really valued about BYRDs. As well as Jennie, we'd have sessions with people like Michel Assouline and Henk van Bergen, and although they all had their own ways of doing things, I'd always learn something. Often I'd go home and my head would be buzzing with all the things I needed to work on, but Judy was always there to help explain things to me if I got stuck or there were things I didn't understand.

On several occasions I was invited to attend squad training, which was a huge honour for me. In the early

2000s the British Young Rider team included Laura Bechtolsheimer, who was Dr B's daughter, and Maria Eilberg. Maria, like Laura and Jennie, had dressage running through her veins: her father was Ferdi, who was hugely respected as a trainer and rider, although brother Michael had decided to follow a career in showjumping.

I never expected to make the team myself because I simply wasn't getting good enough results and Wiz, though he was a fantastic horse, would never be up there with the best. Being an older boy and a school-master he knew the job inside out and had a few tricks up his sleeve: pirouettes I particularly remember because he'd often realise he knew more than I did and take over and spin round on his own.

I don't think Jennie liked Wiz much – she used to call him 'that lazy brute', which really annoyed Judy – but René was properly lazy whereas Wiz would some-times simply say, 'Hmm, not today. I'm not really feeling it today.' Then you'd have to say, 'Oh, come on, Wizzy! Try?' And you could feel him sort of roll his eyes and say, 'Oh, *all right* then.' He was such a gent and always did his best, whereas René was just a pain in the backside.

About this time, I got the ride on a third horse: Lucaro. Luke, like Wiz, was owned by Richard Heley, but he was completely different: smaller and flashier. Judy mostly rode him, but he had one big issue: he wouldn't piaffe. In fact, Peter Storr, the international dressage rider and future judge, had told Judy he couldn't piaffe.

The thing about piaffe is that it's a natural movement: if you hold a stallion while he's trying to get to a mare, he'll start jogging on the spot. The same with passage and flying changes – horses naturally do them all the time when they're out in the field, cantering around. What's not natural is trying to get them to perform movements to order while they're wearing a saddle and bridle and have got a rider on their backs. And, obviously, because you can't talk to a horse, the only way to communicate anything you want it to do is through your legs and seat and reins. That's partly why it takes such a long time to get horses to Grand Prix level: you start with them when they're four, and if you've got a very, very good horse you can be at the top at nine. Most horses won't get there until they're ten or eleven, and they'll then need another two or three years of experience and training before they reach their very best.

With all that in mind, I shouldn't really have thought I could teach Luke to piaffe just like that. But I did feel quite confident and I can never resist a challenge so I told Judy I wanted to have a go. As you can imagine, she looked at me – the apprentice – in total disbelief. 'I bet you can't do it.' 'I bet you I can! I bet you £5 I can.' I realise now how cocky that sounds, and I'd hate to have come across that way, but if somebody says I can't or won't be able to do something it only makes me want to do it more. Anyway, within two weeks I managed to get Lucaro piaffing, at which point Judy kindly let me have the ride on him (although, Judy Harvey, you still owe me my £5). But we all know what pride comes before.

Half Moon Bardolino (Billy) was a bright chestnut seventeen-hand gelding that Judy was training but wanted to sell. I'd ridden him a couple of times and one day when Judy had clients coming she asked me if I'd show him to them. 'Charlotte's been playing with a bit of piaffe,' she said as I was going round the school. 'Why don't you show them, Charlotte?' So I picked up my whip and touched him on the bum, and of course he bucked me clean off. I was so embarrassed. 'He's never done that before,' I said – at which, although it was true, the clients were clearly thinking, yeah, right. But there's nothing you can do in a situation like that except pick yourself up, get back on and carry on as though nothing has happened – although Billy obviously wasn't going anywhere that day.

* * *

In May 2004 I had my first experience of riding abroad at a Young Rider competition in Limburg in the Netherlands with Wiz. We were entered for three tests but I honestly don't remember much about it beyond getting there, which was a whole adventure in itself. Before every foreign show all the riders and their mums would meet at Dover and then drive across the continent in convoy, and as we still had our battered old horsebox my mum and brother spent the entire evening before trying to cover up the worst of the rust patches. From the start, Ian would come along with us to my European shows, partly for moral support and also to keep Mum company. I still went to sleep the moment I got in a horsebox and we started moving, and I'd often wake up to the two of them chuckling because Mum was lost and had gone round a roundabout ten times.

There were two more firsts in 2004: my first taste of riding to music, and my first pas-de-deux. In fact, the two happened together and by accident.

The Horse of the Year Show that year had decided to hold a special, one-off Freestyle competition, with two teams competing to music in an individual Grand Prix kur, a pas-de-deux, and a quadrille. Stephen Clarke and the British Chef d'Equipe David Trott were judging, and the two team captains were Emile Faurie and Nicola

McGivern, who were both Olympic riders. Nicola had invited Anna Ross to be on her team, but then two days before the competition, she'd had to pull out.

Ian needed someone to ride his pas-de-deux with and Richard Heley agreed I could take Wiz, so that was how I found myself, the day before the competition, trying to learn a whole new routine from scratch to the music from *The Full Monty*.

As we were waiting to go into the ring, I made Ian promise he'd tell me which way I should be going because I knew if he didn't, we'd just end up crashing straight into each other. Ian was as good as his word, and although he had to tell me what to do at virtually every stride we actually did a really respectable test. Then the rest of the team did well too, and to our amazement Ian and I found ourselves double winners, of both the individual and team competitions. We were called back into the arena for the prize-giving, occasions I'd loved ever since my showing days, and given our special rosettes and nice Horse of the Year show rugs. Then we were allowed a lap of honour in the spotlight, and at that point Ian's horse Tulip decided she was going to bolt.

Tulip was a chestnut mare, very strong-minded, and quite naughty with Ian. He had been born with scoliosis and would eventually have to give up riding altogether, so sitting on a horse wasn't easy for him. Sitting trot was something he found especially hard and he'd have to do it with his legs stuck out straight in front of him like he was riding with waterskies, and when Tulip took off galloping he didn't always find it easy to stop her.

I was trying not to laugh because it wasn't actually very funny at all, but when Ian started lapping me, petrified and hanging on for dear life, honestly, I could not stop myself. He eventually managed to aim Tulip into a corner, which did the job, and his face when he came out was just a picture. My mum had come up to Birmingham to watch and we both ended up crying with laugher all the way home. Ian took a little bit longer to see the funny side, but I think the case of champagne we won probably helped him get there.

* * *

Fernandez had been backed – that is, he'd had someone lie over his back and start to sit upright on him – but after he'd been out in the field a couple of months I couldn't get straight on him and ride. Very slowly I started lunging him and getting him fit, introducing him to the saddle so he didn't buck, and teaching him the basics. Because he was young and green he was very wobbly, so trying to get him going straight was one of the first challenges. But he was always very forward-thinking and didn't need much leg on him, and because he was so keen and willing to work I had to focus on trying to keep one step ahead of him.

Teaching a young horse is like building a house correctly: if you get your foundations wrong, everything on top is going to be wrong as well. Although I'd helped break horses at home with Mum I'd never really done one properly myself, so Judy would always be with me as eyes on the ground and a source of advice. Whatever the weather, the three of us would be out there, and because there was no indoor school at Judy's, that was a lesson in itself. Summer was bad enough because it would get scorching hot and there'd be no cover anywhere, but winter was worse because if it snowed you'd have to dig the track in around the outside of the school as well as salt all the yard before you even thought about riding. The very worst thing was when it started tipping it down, because Judy would just carry on: she had a little hut at the top of the arena, which had a gas heater in it, and when it rained she'd go in her warm, dry, gas-heated hut and you'd get wet through to your knickers.

Jayne Turney and I would often put the world to rights over the muck heap at Judy's, and that hut was something I remember us both having strong feelings about. We'd rant and rave and meanwhile the muck-heap would get it, which was probably why it was the most picture-perfect muck-heap in the land: it even had stepped levels and square ends. But at competitions, you've got to deal with whatever the situation is: as Judy said, if you're serious there's no point in just being a fair-weather rider, and very right she was, too.

* * *

My next European outing was to Roosendaal in March 2005. This time I had both Luke and Wiz with me and, as it was winter, Mum decided to hire a lorry with heating. Ian was with us again, so he can back me up when I say we woke on the morning of the competition with icicles on our eyelashes. I swear, Roosendaal must have been the coldest place on the planet that week and I absolutely hate being cold: I'd get back to the lorry at shows as a kid, stick the stove on full blast and stand in front of it until I got the feeling back in my legs. When we discovered the gas cylinder had run out, we were not pleased.

While I was riding, Mum had to go off and try to find somewhere that sold gas; then there was another palaver because even when she did manage to communicate what she wanted, the bottle didn't fit the lorry's English connections. I have to say, she didn't miss much. I got a pretty normal 62 per cent with Wiz to finish twenty-eighth in the Young Rider Prix St Georges, but then Lucaro somehow managed to get his tongue over the bit at the very start of his test and the whole rest of the time it was flapping everywhere: he was pretty much licking his eyeballs out. Obviously that's not what the judges want to see, added to which it was so cold I couldn't even feel the reins. We got 58 per cent and ended up thirty-sixth, which was exactly where we should have been.

For me, competing abroad was always exciting, and more about watching new people and gaining experience than winning. The shows I was riding in at home were gradually getting more important, though. In February 2005 I won my first regional title, Novice Champion, with Dez, and in August I competed in my first international with Wow Voyager at Hickstead. This was my biggest competition to date, so I was thrilled to come away with a second, a fourth and a fifth. I'd loved my showing days at Hickstead, but being back there didn't make me miss them: I knew that dressage was what I should be doing.

Autumn and Dez was back in the spotlight again, winning the Brightwells Challenge at Addington. This was a Freestyle competition and I'd put my floorplan together with Judy; the music I'd got off a website. My sister drove me in a tiny blue lorry that was virtually an ice-cream van, and on the way we dreamed about what we might end up doing with all the prize money. It was several thousand pounds in total – far more than I'd ever been in the running for before – but having actually pulled it off, there was no question about it. I'd give it to Mum to help with the bills.

I was loving every moment of riding and competing, but there was a downside: for the first time in my life, I was beginning to struggle with nerves.

My problem was remembering the tests, and the more different tests I started to ride, the worse it got. A couple of times I rode into the arena, had a complete blank and totally forgot where I was going, and once you do that your confidence really goes.

Some riders have callers for their tests, which means you don't have to worry about remembering anything because you've got someone standing there shouting directions. But because callers aren't allowed at regionals or championships, Judy wasn't keen on ever relying on them. She suggested instead that I try a sports psychologist, and as I'd heard a couple speak at BYRDS events, I decided to give it a go. It was a great piece of advice, because after I'd worked with Jenny Killilea my nerves never really troubled me again.

With Jenny, I learned quite quickly that the way to solve problems was to break them down. She'd write down what I told her was worrying me, and the weird thing is that when you see things written down on paper, they don't seem as bad anymore: you look at them and think, 'What am I worrying about?'

One of the main reasons why I'd get so flustered and stressed at shows was because I was always rushing against time, so Jenny made me come up with a plan. The night before a competition, I had to write down everything from when I had to get up and what time I was going to plait my horse, to when I wanted to leave the yard and when I needed to be warmed up by. I also had to allow extra time for if things went wrong. Simply not having to carry it all in my head allowed me to get back to focusing on what was important. More difficult to deal with was the reason why I was rushing around in the first place.

I'd gradually begun to find that Mum, who'd become used to helping me, was now trying to help me a bit too much. She'd always be with me in the warm-up arena, and because she was worrying about turning my horse out perfectly – which matters in showing but not so much in dressage – my warm-ups were getting shorter. I'd be late getting on my horse, and then I'd panic because I didn't have enough time to prepare, and that's when I'd start stressing and forgetting things. Judy had always pushed me to grow up and be more independent, but I knew that Mum felt that being there supporting me was her role. She'd always wanted her own parents to come and watch her ride and they'd never been interested, so from her perspective she was giving me something she hadn't had.

It was a difficult position for me to be in because I knew Mum had given up her career to have us kids: she'd given us the chance to do what she would have wanted to do herself. But I also knew that Judy was right and I had to start being more independent.

Asking Mum to take a step back wasn't a great conversation for either of us, and because I was young I didn't really soften the blow. She'd seen Judy taking me under her wing and the two of us going off and doing things without her, which I know made her feel as though she was losing me; she also found it hard to accept that I still wanted Ian around helping me. The thing is that, as everybody knows, mother–daughter relationships aren't easy: mothers can unfortunately say the wrong things at the wrong time, and although you don't mean to, you snap back. Ian could say things to me about my riding that my mum never could. I knew she wanted to look after me and help where possible, and I tried to explain that I wasn't stopping her from coming to watch me because I still really valued her support, but I didn't want her to groom for me and be there with me all the time.

It wasn't an easy transition for either of us, and although Mum's slowly settled more into the spectator role, to this day it's a delicate balancing act and one that's hard for us both.

* * *

I'd been with Judy for two or three years when Roland left and I took over from him as her travelling groom. It was great for me because I was only competing at low-level shows myself, whereas with Judy I'd be going to shows where I'd see all the top riders. I'm the kind of person who wants to learn and take in information whenever and wherever they can, so watching the people I aspired to be like – Carl Hester included – was amazing for me.

I was never made to feel like an outsider at those big competitions, although I knew I was one at that point. Often I'd feel quite shy amongst the kind of riders Judy was competing with, and it seemed very much like a world where everybody knew everybody. The fact that Judy was a judge and commentator as well as a rider meant that people like Carl would often turn up at the yard, and I'd always be completely in awe of him when I saw him. He had that effect on a lot of other people, too.

The smaller, Premier League shows that I was competing at had their own crowd – Nicky Patrick, Holly Borough, Anne-Marie Perry and Henry Boswell. Henry was always our entertainer, and I used to be astonished that he could have such a good night, shall we say, and still do so well when he had to ride the next day. There was one evening when he'd had a glass or two and couldn't find his phone anywhere; the next morning, I saw he'd got it again and it turned out he'd put it in the fridge in his lorry.

By now I was twenty, so it seemed like high time I learned to drive, getting around being another thing I'd been relying on my mum and sister for. I had lessons with my brother – he sat in the back while I drove, and then we swapped – and as he was so into cars he was much better at it than I was. Because I'm the kind of person I am, I can't stand being bad at anything, and it especially annoyed me since Charles is younger than me. The first time I took my test I was ridiculously nervous. We were in Bletchley, a really busy part of town, and I had an old grump examining me who sat there in silence. At some point I pulled out without indicating, so of course I failed. For the next attempt I got a really lovely guy who chatted to me the whole way, and when he passed me I felt like I was a free person at last – all I needed to do now was decide where I was going.

I'd been at Judy's for four years and I think we both felt the time had come for a change. I wanted to be riding more, and from going to so many shows with her I'd also seen lots of different trainers, using lots of different techniques that I wanted to try out myself.

In July, I took Wiz to a small international in Le Touquet, and on the ferry on the way back, I remember saying to Caroline Griffiths, the BYRDS National Training Coordinator, 'I don't know what I'm going to do.' It's amazing now to think how soon and how totally my life was to change.

* * *

The first time I saw Valegro was at Addington in the summer of 2006. He was being ridden by Carl, who also owned him, and I can honestly say I was blown away. His canter was huge, absolutely huge, and even though it looked a bit out of control, he looked like he'd be so much fun to ride.

One of the things that immediately jumped out about him was the way he was built: he was a complete and utter powerhouse. Nowadays you see a lot of thorough-bred-type dressage horses with very elegant, long legs, but Valegro was much more of an old-fashioned, stocky stamp – a real-leg-in-each-corner type. He completely filled your eye, but he also had a pretty, dished face like a seahorse's, and even then he looked like he only wanted to please.

I saw him again, a few months later, at the Nationals, where he won the Shearwater Four-Year-Old Championship. He left the same impression on me as last time – here was a horse that stood out from all the rest. Dez and I were entered for the Elementary class at the Nationals where we finished third, which was a good result because as we were warming up it started to rain. Not just a little bit of rain, but torrential, thundering, lightning, fill-your-boots-up-with-water rain. My boots actually did fill up with water and I could feel it sloshing all round my legs; my saddle was so slippery I couldn't sit on it, I could hardly hold my reins, and Dez was curling up like a hedgehog because he wanted to get out of it so badly. There wasn't a single part of me that was dry, the arenas were all underwater and everything and everybody was soaked.

I carried on warming up, trying to make the best of it, but then suddenly the class was suspended: the judges, who were sitting in their cars around the arena, had had their ignitions on so they could use their windscreen wipers, but it had been raining so hard for so long that their batteries had all gone flat.

It was brilliant timing for me. I ran back to the stables, dried Fernandez off and got him a new saddle-cloth, then tried to dry myself. My coat was too wet to put back on, but I managed to borrow someone else's; I somehow then managed to change my breeches, empty the water out of my boots, pull myself together, get myself back on and still be in the arena by the time the judges were ready to go again. It carried on raining throughout my test and we were sloshing through puddles with water sheeting up around us the whole time – I might as well have been riding on the beach. But all those days of getting soaked to the skin with Judy had obviously done something for me, and 68 per cent in those circumstances felt like a really good score.

The year as a whole had been a good one for Dez and me. It had begun in February when we'd won a Novice class at Addington Winter Regional with 73 per cent and finished second in the Freestyle with 77 per cent. At the winter championships a few months later we finished second in a Novice class with 69 per cent and won the Freestyle with 71 per cent; at Windmill Farm in May, we won two Elementary classes with 74 per cent and 75 per cent; and then at Hickstead in July we took the Six-Year-Old Young Horse Championship with a score of 79 per cent.

I'd always felt Dez was a star but now he was starting to look like one, and other people were thinking so too. Not long after the Nationals a letter arrived from British Dressage inviting me to bring Dez to a selection day run by the Equestrian World Class Performance Programme.

World Class is a Lottery-funded organisation whose mission is to identify and develop talent and deliver success 'on the world stage'. In 2006 a new World Class scheme, the Equine Pathway Programme, aimed at developing young horses that might go on to compete for Britain, was introduced. To have Dez, who I'd trained myself from the beginning, recognised as a potential World Class horse was incredible for me. It was a big wide world out there and I often felt very much like a little fish in a huge pond, so to be singled out in that way was really special.

The selection day for the Pathway was held at Addington and the selectors were David Trott and Richard Davison, who was then the Dressage Equine Pathway Manager. Two riders had also been invited to attend and give their opinions: Emile Faurie and Carl Hester. Before we started I'd had to sign a form giving consent for either Carl or Emile to try Dez, and all I could think as I ticked the box was how much I'd love to see Carl Hester ride my horse. I was so desperate to do well, and for Dez to do well, but when Carl actually did come over and ask if he could have a sit on him, I was lost for words. Then I looked down and saw the spurs Carl was wearing: they weren't sharp, but they were quite long. Fernandez being as sensitive as he was, I was a bit taken aback, but I couldn't exactly tell Carl Hester to be careful with his legs. It was one of those moments where you think to yourself, 'Just shut up! Shut up! Don't say anything!' but I had to really bite my tongue because so far nobody had ridden Dez other than me. Anyway, away Carl went while I stood there watching, rooted to the spot. It was so exciting seeing him on my horse, although I was nervous too because I had no idea what he was thinking.

After a bit, Carl came back, dismounted, and handed me Dez's reins. 'He's very sensitive,' he said. But the overall verdict was that Dez was a lovely horse: that I'd done a super job of training him and that he showed great potential for the Grand Prix work, including piaffe. Which, as you can imagine, had me beaming from ear to ear: I was so pleased Dez had gone well for another rider and hadn't let me down.

My parents were in Portugal on holiday at the time, and as soon as we'd finished I rang Mum to tell her the news. 'Mum, Carl rode Dez! I've kissed the saddle and now I'm never going to clean it ever again!' I was acting like a little kid and I knew it, but I was so excited I couldn't help myself.

When Dez was selected for the Pathway, it felt like a massive step forward: the first rung on the ladder and confirmation that both of us were on the right track. But although one of the benefits was that I would be invited to training days at the Unicorn Trust Equestrian Centre in Stow-on-the-Wold, I still needed to find someone who'd work with me day to day.

The next time I saw Carl was at an Addington Premier League show, and it was then that Mum approached him to ask if he'd consider giving me some lessons – I made her do it because I was too afraid to do it myself. I stood there watching them, thinking: 'Mum's talking to Carl! Oh my God, Mum's talking to Carl!' And when she came back I still couldn't believe she'd gone and done it.

Carl was too busy to teach me at that point in time, but he suggested I stay in touch and finally, in January 2007, a space opened up in his diary. He was then based up in Gloucestershire at Court Farm, which belonged to Anne Seifert-Cohn, and even though I was so excited I still managed to sleep all the way there.

It must have been after our third lesson that I finally got up the courage to ask Carl if he needed anyone – if not staff, then maybe someone to do a bit of work experience. The look on my face when he said yes must have been priceless. Carl's head girl, Caroline Dawson, was going on holiday for ten days. If I wanted to, I could bring Fernandez and be a temporary working pupil. I wouldn't get paid, but Fernandez could stay for free and we'd have lessons from Carl.

I didn't need to think twice: Mum helped me sort out Dez and get all his stuff ready, I got all mine ready, and that was it, we were off. As it turned out, I went for ten days and never came back.

5

Meant to Be

MANY PEOPLE HAVE asked why I think Carl gave me the opportunity he did. He was a world-class trainer and rider, the person everyone looked up to, and he was literally inundated every day with people asking him for a job.

My natural balance and feel were, I think, something he felt he could work with, and from the start Carl said that I had a gift for teaching horses the collected movements. Our mentalities were similar, too: I'm self-motivated and wanted to ride everything, which was how Carl had been when he was starting out in his career. When I arrived, he was at a low point in his personal life and wondering about retiring, and I think my being so enthusiastic and driven to learn meant he appreciated having me around. And just being in the right place at the right time was part of it, as well – which, looking back, seems to have happened a lot in my life.

As a kid it had been horrible having to leave the house I'd loved and grown up in and move from place to place all the time. We'd never know where we were going next, and Mum and I would always be worrying if we could find good yards where we could afford to put the ponies. I wouldn't change it now, though, because if we hadn't moved around so much I would never have met Rory or Ian, and without Ian I wouldn't have met Judy and gone to her.

I'd worked and grafted my absolute hardest to be where I was, but it seems crazy to think now that I've never once in my life had a job interview. It's almost as though everything that's happened has happened for a reason – like stepping stones all the way along.

The chance to learn from Carl and benefit from his knowledge and experience was an amazing one for me, but he'd asked me to do a job and working for Carl meant you worked hard. Even harder, if it were possible, than in my previous job. At Judy's there had been ten or twelve horses to look after; at Carl's there were twenty odd. It was also a competition yard, not a livery yard, so the pace was flat out.

There were four of us including Lucy Cartwright, Carl's under-rider, and our day started with feeding and mucking out at 7 a.m. We'd still be mucking out when Carl and Spencer Wilton, Carl's partner and another professional dressage rider, arrived to start riding at 8.30 a.m. You had to stop, get their horses ready, then go back to the mucking out, but you also had to be ready to stop again the second they'd finished riding so you could wash off their horses. Once all the mucking out was done, the horses Carl and Spencer weren't riding had to be ridden, but you still had to make sure you were ready to tack up and untack if either of them needed you. The whole day it carried on like that – it was absolutely manic. I'd never worked like it in my life before.

As soon as the horses had all been ridden they had to be turned out, and that took ages because the fields were a long way from the yard. Then if one of them decided to go crazy and start galloping around, you'd have Carl shouting at you to go and get it back in and take one of the others out. Off you'd go, traipsing through the mud to catch it – which was hell because it was winter – and of course they'd have found the muddiest part of the field to roll in and turned into an absolute hippo. So then you'd have to wash it off again, and your hands would freeze with all the cold water. I often get asked about my false nails but the real reason I started wearing them was because I was trying to disguise my old lady hands and arthritic knuckles, which I've got from years of working outside in the wet and cold.

We stopped for lunch for an hour between one and two, then the afternoon was all about yard duties and cleaning tack.

Tack cleaning was one of Spencer's things and he was very fussy about it: he said that if you didn't clean the bridle properly, including taking the bit off, the leather got stiff because there'd still be muck stuck in the loops. That's very true, but then you weren't allowed to put the bits back on the bridles until the moment they were needed. Why you couldn't was beyond me, because when Spenny or Carl suddenly announced they wanted their horse ready, there'd be a real panic: not only did you have to get it groomed and bandaged, you also had to fiddle around with putting the bit back on before you could tack up. It seemed completely impractical to me, but it was one of Spencer's rules so I wasn't going to question it.

There were moments sometimes when I just wanted to stand in the middle of that yard and scream, 'I've only got one pair of hands!' But then Carl would ask me to warm up one of his top horses and I'd be so excited I'd forget how exhausted I was.

The first time Carl put me on his Grand Prix horse Pro-Set, I was terrified. I was convinced I was going to ruin him because I didn't know what I was doing, especially when Carl announced he was going to teach me one-time changes.

With four-, three- and two- tempi changes, which were all I'd previously done, you've got time to think about your aids. With one-time changes, you can't wait for your horse to land before you ask it to change legs because, if you do, it's too late and you've missed the moment. As a rider that means you just have to keep moving your legs backwards and forwards in rhythm with your horse even though you're not sure what they're doing under you, which feels really bizarre.

The pressure I felt to get it right in front of Carl was incredible. I didn't want him to think I was useless, but a voice in my head was telling me over and over I couldn't do it. Sure enough, I kept getting it for a couple of strides and then losing it again.

It was so frustrating, but every other day Carl would put me back on Pro-Set and encourage me to have a go. I can't remember how many attempts it took me, but when I did eventually get it I was straight on the phone. 'Mum, you'll never guess what I've just done!'

The whole of those ten days I spent trying to absorb everything I could from watching Carl. If I had any spare time I'd go and listen to him teaching other riders and sit there trying to take in as much information as possible so I could put it into practice in my own riding. Every second I felt like I was totally living my dream, but I also knew it was a dream that was going to come to an end: as soon as Caroline came back from her holiday, Carl would be sending me home.

Actually, it was Spenny who I was expecting to send me off: he was generally the one responsible for keeping people in line. Carl has never enjoyed confrontation, and maybe that's partly why things happened like they did, because it got to day eleven, Caroline came back, and everything pretty much carried on as before. There was no letter, no sit-down formal meeting, no discussion of pay – to this day Carl has never paid me a wage. It just slowly dawned on me that Dez and I were staying put. Since I'd been working for Carl, I'd been living with Lucy in Anne Seifert-Cohn's house. We had our own bedrooms and a bathroom, and in the evenings Lucy and I would go down to Anne's kitchen and cook dinner together. I'll never forget that house because it used to be absolutely freezing: when you've been working outside all day all you want is to come in to somewhere warm and Anne never put the heating on. After a bit Lucy and I decided we were going to get our own little electric heaters, which we hid under our beds during the day so Anne wouldn't see them. We'd get them out each evening and stick them on full blast, have a shower, then literally sit in front of them, holding our towels open to try and warm up. We knew we were being naughty and always worried in case Anne came in and wanted to know why it was so hot, so eventually we decided we'd just have to lie and say we'd had both of our hairdryers going. Seriously, I think it would have killed Anne if she'd known how much of her electricity we were actually burning.

Lucy was more experienced than I was, so if I didn't understand something I could ask her questions, but the two of us were friends as well as colleagues. When you work and live with someone it can be difficult, but it never felt like that with Lucy: we cooked together, ate together, shopped together, did practically everything together. We also used to go out drinking together in Cheltenham, but at the time Lucy liked a bit of a party whereas I was mostly just exhausted. After a day's work I'd get back to my room and want to do nothing except lie on my bed and chill out, whereas Lucy would go out every Wednesday and on Friday and Saturday too. I'd struggle to get through the day even if I'd had a good night's sleep, but Lucy could go out and be bright as a button next morning. Sometimes it'd get to around midday and she'd suddenly go a bit green, but it never got in the way of her work, and if Carl or anyone else came over she'd be absolutely perfect again.

Because I was so close to my mum, I don't think Judy thought I'd last away from home. I always wanted to go back to visit at weekends and on my days off, but it was probably worse for Mum than it was for me: she's quite an emotional person, and there'd be tears rolling down her face when I left. What was nice for me was that if I was missing people at home or had had a bad day, I could always go and sit with Dez for comfort. It was so cool having him with me again instead of at a livery yard: in the mornings I could wake up and go and see him, or go and check on him in the evening and have night cuddles.

Being at Carl's was a bit like walking into a sweet shop for me: I'd never seen so many nice horses in one yard. As well as Pro-Set, there were Lecantos, TMovistar and Dolendo, who were all Grand Prix horses, then lots of other youngsters like Uthopia. There was also the horse that had wowed me so much at the National Championships: Valegro.

I'd seen him once more since that day, when I'd come up to Carl's with Mum and Dez for a lesson. Lucy was cantering him round the outdoor school, and they went down the long side in about four strides, Valegro's stride was so massive. At that point I already knew Lucy slightly from riding at the same shows, and so when she'd finished I went over and said, 'Does that feel as amazing as it looks?' She didn't need to think twice.

All of Carl's young horses were given fruit and vege-table stable names, and getting Blueberry – as Valegro was known – ready for Carl or Lucy to ride was all part of a normal day. There was no question of me riding him as I was only a working pupil and the new girl, but I'd be getting him in and out from the field, tacking him up, brushing him, mucking him out and, the most important job of all if you were Blueberry, feeding him.

Food was always his top priority. From day one, unless you had treats for him, he wasn't interested. I swear it's why I get on so well with him: we can both be bribed by food. Blueberry would eat anything – sugar, carrots, apples, bananas, bread – and when you put him out in the field he was like a hoover. He'd have a buck and a kick and then his head would be straight down and he'd eat and eat and eat and eat. If you saw him come up to draw breath, you were lucky.

If you didn't have anything for him, on the other hand, he could be a bit unsociable. Even having his rug put on, he'd put his ears back. I'd been used to Dez, who was a real people person: you'd be mucking Dez out and he'd be all over you, nuzzling your pockets to find out if you'd got any treats and banging the stable door to get you back if you walked away. For years I tried and tried to make Blueberry more cuddly and kissy like Dez, but he was just never that sort of horse. You'd give him a hug and he'd give you a 'Please don't do that' kind of look. He always knew what he wanted, Blueberry, and that was his own personal space. However, when I arrived at Carl's yard in January 2007, he himself was unwanted.

Blueberry's story had begun on 5 July 2002 when he was born on Burgh Haamstede, an island in the Netherlands. His breeders, Maartje and Joop Hanse, decided to call him 'Vainqueurfleur', which was a combination of his mother's name, Maifleur, and 'vainquer', which is French for victor. Valegro's sire was the black dressage stallion Negro, and it was from Negro that Valegro got his stockiness and short, strong legs.

Vainqueurfleur became Valegro when he was sold as a colt to Gertjan van Olst, Negro's owner. Gertjan's wife, Anne, was an international rider and sometimes trained with Carl, and while Carl was visiting Holland in 2005, Anne took him to see the KWPN stallion show and grading. One young horse particularly caught Carl's eye, and that turned out to be Valegro – even then, as Carl says, he had 'the head of a duchess and the bottom of a cook'. But although he obviously had massive power in his hindquarters, it seemed at the time that Valegro was never going to be big and special enough to keep as a stallion for breeding. He was gelded, and because he wasn't expensive, Carl decided to buy him.

Back in Gloucestershire, Carl sent Valegro to his friend Sandra Biddlecombe – the same Sandra Biddlecombe from whom Mum and I had bought René – to be broken. Sandra's farm is a short drive from Carl's, and she had Valegro with her until the summer before I came to the yard.

Valegro's career had got off to a winning start with the Four-Year-Old Championship, and he'd also won the 2006 Badminton Young Dressage Horse of the Future title, but nobody knew what would happen next. He was small and squat, just over sixteen hands, so for Carl – who is well over six foot – he was far from ideal. His canter was also so massive it hurt Carl's back, which was already bad, while his other paces were pretty normal: to begin with, it was only in canter that Blueberry looked like such an amazing horse.

Even before I arrived Carl had already tried to sell him twice, once to a friend, Suzanne Davies, and once back to the Van Olsts. Neither had worked out: Suzanne had got a tax bill she wasn't expecting and couldn't afford to go through with the sale, and the Van Olsts told Carl he should really keep Blueberry as they thought he was going to turn out to be good.

Carl decided to take their advice for the time being, but because he found Blueberry uncomfortable to ride, he let Lucy have the ride on him. Lucy, is tiny though – only 5'2" – and Blueberry was starting to get too strong for her.

One day, a month or two after I arrived at Carl's, Lucy and I were having a lesson with him. Blueberry was pulling Lucy around like a rag doll and as I'm taller than her at 5' 6", Carl told us to swap: Lucy got on the horse I was riding, and I got on Blueberry.

From that first moment I loved him, absolutely loved him. He was fiery, he was sensitive, he was expressive, he was powerful – everything I'd always wanted in a horse, he was. It felt like he was the missing piece I had been looking for. You know when you get on a horse whether you like it or you don't, but Blueberry gave me a feeling I'd never experienced before: there was such a strong connection between us straight away. Even his shape was part of it. When you sit on Blueberry you really feel like you're part of him because he's so solid and built like a barrel – your legs wrap right the way round. You've got a good length of neck in front of you, but behind you you've got hind legs pounding like pistons, almost too much for the front end to cope with. The power was like nothing I'd ever felt in my life: when I asked for canter it felt as if we were going to take off. Some horses canter and just cover the ground, but with Blueberry you were actually leaving the floor, the moment of suspension was so long. The only thing I can compare it to is a rollercoaster: it gave me that same thrill in the pit of my stomach, the buzz of going so fast it was almost like losing control.

Even then, I could feel how much I could achieve with him: this was my perfect dance partner. But when I first started riding Valegro the real problem wasn't so much his lack of size or his unruliness as his head shaking, and it was so serious that Carl was beginning to think he might not even have a career.

Nobody really knows what causes head shaking, or how to cure it. Carl had tried all sorts of medicines, had all sorts of specialists out and had even thought about having Blueberry operated on, but what it seemed to come down to was that he was so sensitive to everything. Nothing could touch Blueberry's skin: metal buckles would sometimes give him a rash so we'd have to make sure there was a cloth over them to protect him. In the summer he'd get hay fever and his eyes would start running; even extra-strong mints would make his nose run. He'd eat the mint, which he loved, but then he'd get stressed because his nose would run and tickle his face, and that would set his head shaking off. Flies had the same effect: if one even slightly touched his face or nose he'd strike out with his leg or shake his head violently.

I was always trying to pick up on every little thing that might trigger it, because you'd be with him and he'd be trying to bang his head or rub his face with his legs or drag his nose up the walls. It was so bad that Carl had even tried radionics, which is a form of complementary therapy. Horse people sometimes call radionics 'the black box', because you give a sample of your horse's hair to a radionics practitioner, who takes it away and puts in a black, box-like machine. The idea is that they then use 'radionic therapy' to perform a kind of energy healing – you never actually see them do it and your horse doesn't have to be present, you just pay your £20 a month and the problem is meant to get better.

Carl is not at all the sort of person who believes in that kind of thing and many people think it's a myth, but there did seem to be some change in Blueberry after we started him on it so Carl decided to keep it going. With time, we found out that putting Blueberry in a double bridle helped too. Normally, you put a double bridle on a horse when they're six, coming seven, because until then their teeth are changing; it's also important that you can still get them listening and responding in just a snaffle. Blueberry was five and a half, but the curb chain definitely seemed to make a difference: it lies on an acupuncture pressure point, and although straightforward acupuncture hadn't worked for Blueberry, with the curb chain on he did seem to be more relaxed. What's more, it gave me more control over him, which in turn made him less nervous – Blueberry was the kind of horse who, if he didn't feel like his rider was in charge, would start to worry.

Even with all his problems I could feel the talent in him, and Carl knew it was there too. But in 2007 he had other horses to concentrate on and it didn't seem like Blueberry was going to be the one for him. Spencer didn't get on with Blueberry either, and even though I had such a good connection with him, I felt I couldn't come out and say how special I thought he was – the only way I could persuade Carl he was worth keeping was for me to actually show it. Which is when fate stepped in again. In March, Carl was due to be away in Spain for three weeks competing on what's known as the 'Sunshine Tour'. It would be three weeks when I could focus on working with Blueberry and, I hoped, prove just how good he was.

6

Love and Heartbreak

IT SOUNDS FUNNY, but the problem with Blueberry was that he tried so hard. Rather than waiting and listening to my aids, he was always trying to jump ahead, and then when he didn't understand what I wanted him to do, he'd get tense: it was all go, go, go, and no whoa, whoa, whoa. Tension would always make Blueberry's head shaking worse, and the more I tried to figure him out, the more I realised it was almost like a form of Tourette's: his work ethic was incredible, but his brain was constantly on overdrive. Sometimes all you wanted was to tell him to take a breath and slow down.

There were two arenas at Anne's, indoor and outdoor. The indoor was smaller, so that's where I rode Blueberry: with less space and four walls round him, it was easier to keep him under control.

As well as working to make him more relaxed, I was also trying to get him more supple: tension would make him tight and while some horses get stiff in their mouths and necks, with Blueberry it was his whole body that would go rigid. I concentrated on lots of easy, basic transitions and simple exercises – things that he could cope with and wouldn't get him stressed – and the more relaxed he was, the better he got.

'Come on, Blueberry!' I'd say every time I got on him. 'We need it to be a good day today!' Every day when there wasn't an improvement felt like a day nearer the time Carl might get rid of him, but every week I could

81

see a difference. By the time Carl came back Blueberry was much more on the bit and not so stiff, and I'd also managed to slow down his canter. I was so proud and excited to show Carl what I'd done, and to my relief he agreed there'd been a change. But I'd realised by now that unless I actually came out and said something, he wasn't going to know how much I cared, and might still end up selling Blueberry. If I was going to have a chance to make him the horse I knew he could be, I was going to have to ask for it.

At this point simply speaking to Carl, let alone asking him something so huge, was a massive deal for me. I'm sure he will laugh if he's reading this because I'm such a chatty person and normally never shut up, but I used to be so nervous trying to talk to him I'd almost choke.

There was a long concrete drive up to Anne's yard, with fields and a canter track on one side. We would walk the horses up the drive before and after work, and when I first started at Carl's I'd try and finish schooling at the same time as him so we'd ride up it together and I'd maybe get to have a few words with him.

Every time it happened, it felt like another giant leap: 'Wow! I'm having a *conversation* with Carl Hester now!' But he was still my boss and the one making all the calls. Who was I to be asking him to keep a horse for me? Much as I wanted to beg and plead with him, I was a nobody – just the working pupil. All I knew was that what I had with Blueberry was special and although he wasn't *a* perfect horse, he was *my* perfect horse. I'd already made a difference to him in the short time we'd had together, and I wanted to keep going so badly and felt so desperate inside that I was going to have to pluck up the courage and say it. 'Please, please, can you not sell him? I just want a chance.'

As I've said, I do believe in fate. Obviously, Carl wasn't about to give Blueberry to me, but after we talked he agreed I could compete him at the lower levels (which, as an international rider, Carl couldn't do anyway). It wasn't a promise, but it was the opportunity of a lifetime – one I'll never stop being grateful for.

Riding Blueberry and riding Dez was like driving two different cars. Blueberry was the Ferrari that you had to learn how to control, and Dez was like a Rolls-Royce. With Blueberry, you'd ask for a flying change and then feel like you were taking off because it was so ginormous, whereas Dez's movements were all smooth and neat. Nothing you ever asked felt like it was a struggle for Dez, it was all comfortable and easy, but the challenge with him was bringing out the wow factor that Blueberry naturally had.

As Dez was a year ahead of Blueberry and that much easier to ride, it was easier for Carl to teach me new movements on Dez and for me then to transfer what I'd learned to Blueberry. I was still riding many of Carl's other horses too – an opportunity worth its weight in gold – and that range of experience was exactly what I needed. It wasn't just about learning the tricks, either: so many things you'd probably never notice or think about are important in dressage.

For example, when you're riding a test, you're making half-halts all the way through. Everybody's definition of a half-halt is different but they're basically a way of rebalancing your horse, which is important because at Grand Prix, with movements coming up so fast, you haven't got a lot of time or space to set things up. To most people they'd be invisible, but that kind of fine-tuning and attention to detail is what makes all the difference at the top, and although half-halts are one of the things I'd learned at the beginning, it wasn't until I got to Carl's that I really understood them. With him, I was also understanding the importance of timing: if you correct a horse it has to be at the right moment, because if you do it too late the horse misunderstands. But as much as Carl's teaching, it was actually being able to sit down and keep watching and watching him every day that was the biggest help – it's one thing having someone tell you what to do, but sometimes it's not until you watch it being done that you really grasp it.

Carl had always thought Dez was a cool little horse, and one day when we were out hacking he suggested, in passing, that we swap: he would have Dez and I could have Valegro. I still don't know if he was serious, but as I saw it, I already had the best of both worlds: I had the ride on Blueberry, who I loved, and in Dez I also owned a horse who was looking like he could be a prospect for London 2012.

Back in 2007, the London Olympics still felt a very, very long way away. At the most recent Olympics in Athens in 2004, the British team of Carl, Richard Davison, Emma Hindle and Nicola McGivern had finished seventh; the Netherlands, Germany and Spain had taken gold, silver and bronze. In the individual competition, Anky had won gold, and Carl had been the highest-placed British rider, finishing twelfth on Peanuts (Escapado).

Carl's focus was now on Beijing in 2008, but for me it was all about London, and in May 2007 Dez and I were invited by the Pathway Programme to take part in a master class for horses that might have Olympic potential. It was held at the Royal Windsor Horse Show and hosted by Richard Davison and David Trott, and I can remember David telling the crowd they were looking at a combination for London 2012.

Did that actually seem like a possibility to me at the time? No, not at all. But I'm the kind of person who always has to set myself goals and when I got to Carl's I set myself three. The first was to ride on a team with him, because he was the best there was and the rider who had motivated and inspired me from the start. The second was to ride at the London Olympia Horse Show, because that was the only major show that, as a child, I'd never managed to qualify for. But the biggest goal was to ride at London 2012 and I can't tell you how much I wanted it – although I knew that just wanting it wasn't enough: if it was going to happen, I was going to have to go out and fight for it. It wouldn't be easy, but I knew I wasn't going to let anything stand in my way. Then things took a turn that I really hadn't planned on.

People often say these things happen when you're least expecting them, and I definitely wasn't looking to find the love of my life when I turned up to a show at Addington in June 2007. Dean Golding, on the other hand, was there to do just that – he was looking for a girlfriend and thought a horse show was a good place to start.

The plan had been cooked up the night before, when Dean met Carl at a dinner party. It had been organised by Carl's friends, Dan and Jamie Greenwood, who were regulars in the pub in Chipping Norton that Dean's dad owned. Dean didn't know anything about dressage, but Carl had invited him to come along and watch him ride the next day and Dean, spotting an opportunity, had agreed. Unfortunately, his scheme then nearly backfired, because when I saw him talking to Carl I thought he must be gay: the number of single straight guys at shows who are friends of Carl's you can count on one hand.

Nevertheless, I liked his deep voice and South African accent, and when I'd ridden Blueberry and went back to say goodbye to Carl, I found the two of them were still chatting. Despite Carl deciding to pull my leg and insist that, hands off, he was keeping Dean for himself, I finally realised Dean was interested in me and we managed to exchange numbers.

A few weeks later, Mum, Dad and I were on holiday in Portugal. I hadn't thought any more about what had happened at Addington, but on the second day we were away, 13 July, I got a text message wishing me happy birthday. The number was Dean's, but at the time I would have sworn it was Carl or Spencer winding me up. 'Right,' I thought, 'I'm calling your bluff,' so I texted back daring whoever it was to come and meet me at my mum's house the Sunday we got back.

We flew home, Sunday arrived, a steel-grey Clio turned up at my mum's house and Dean got out. What he didn't know was that there was an entire welcoming committee lying in wait: my sister and brother, my brother's girlfriend and Jayne Turney had all been visiting and stayed around because they wanted to get a look.

As for me, I'd spent the entire day panicking about what I was going to wear. Smart or casual? Jeans or not jeans? Hair up or hair down? Curly or straight? I was getting more and more nervous until I realised Dean had only seen me once before and that had been when I was looking my absolute worst: there are no hiding places when you're wearing breeches, especially – of all colours – white ones. After that I felt better, although I still wanted to get Dean out of the house and to myself as quickly as possible because, let's face it, parents do have a way of totally and utterly embarrassing you.

We managed to escape for a walk with the dogs, and it was then I found out Dean had only recently moved to England to be with his dad. (Dean's parents had

I was never one for sitting still!

Below: With Mum's passion for horses, it wasn't surprising that both my sister Emma-Jayne and I were hooked almost instantly. My first pony ride – aged only 6 months!

When we weren't jumping the horses, we were jumping the dogs!

Below: Because we were on the road so much during the summer, holidays weren't a top priority for us but I did love visiting my grandfather in Portugal.

Showing was like one big adventure.

Friday could never come quickly enough throughout my entire time at school – I just wanted to ride!

Riding and showing was everything to us.

Left: Me, aged 4 years old on my show pony Toy Grendier.

Below: British Show Pony of the Year, me and Ardenhall Royal Secret.

Top right: Horse of the Year Show riding Oldmere Dylan.

Below right: Horse of the Year Show on Greenfields Pride.

As soon as I was on a horse, it was like being granted my freedom. I would start riding and all my worries would just melt away.

Below: Emma-Jayne and I didn't compete much against each other but we still argued all the time about who'd won what.

Facing page: Ian has been with me on every step of my journey – here we are performing a pas-de-deux at the 2004 Horse of the Year Show.

I'd never been the type of person who was interested in going out at weekends, but sometimes you've got to let your hair down.

Below: For me it's always been about the horses. Here riding Wow Voyager.

divorced when he was young; his mother is South African, and was still living there.) Dean was working in his dad's pub at the time, but he was also a serious runner, which suited me because it meant he knew about the hours and discipline being a sportsperson involved. It didn't take me long to realise I'd found my soulmate, but I still told Dean that, as far as I was concerned, my horses would always come first. Fortunately he accepted that and, having done the entire meet-the-parents shebang on our very first day as a couple, it felt like everything after that would be plain sailing.

* * *

Because people have always seen Blueberry winning medals and breaking records they find it hard to believe he wasn't scoring tens across the board from the start. In young horse classes he never scored that highly for his trot, though: he loved trot and canter extensions because he could just power off, but if you'd seen his normal trot back then, there wasn't a lot to it. His bouncy, spilling-over-with-energy walk cost him marks, too. He was always so eager to be doing the next thing that the slightest touch of your leg would set him off, but then when you asked him to walk, he didn't know what to do with himself. Walk would always be Blueberry's most expensive pace in terms of marks, because rather than being relaxed he'd be like a cat on hot bricks, bouncing up and down. He loved his job so much you could feel him thinking: 'What should I do? I'm meant to be doing something! What is it?' Then you'd pick up your reins ready for the transition and he'd be so keen to go he'd almost start to piaffe.

Young horse classes are marked differently from other tests: the judges are looking at the horse's paces and ability to demonstrate submission and potential, rather than at the way you ride movements. With the exception of the Six-Year-Old Championship, Fernandez had never done that well in young horse classes because he had three nice paces as opposed to three really big ones, and every time I used to come away disappointed we hadn't got the score I thought he deserved.

What I've learned since is that you don't need those big paces in a young Grand Prix horse, just three correct paces you can train. It's not often that horses who are really big movers and scoring tens when they're young go on to have long careers, simply because of all the wear and tear on their bodies. Good Grand Prix horses can also be quite tense when they're young because they're hot and want to be going forward, and that again can cause them to score less well in terms of submission – as Blueberry demonstrated very nicely at our first show together.

We were entered in a young horse class at Hunters Equestrian in Cirencester in the summer of 2007, and the day before when I looked at the test I realised there was a halt-rein back in it. I'd never done one of those before on Blueberry, and because he was so strong I wasn't very confident that going backwards would be something he was going to agree to.

Anyway, Carl and I set about teaching him, me on Blueberry standing next to a wall to keep him straight, Carl tapping his front legs with a whip, and eventually he managed to do it, but he was absolutely dragging himself: he was leaning his whole weight into my hand and he was completely locked in his jaw.

We decided it would have to do, and on the day it turned out to be the least of my worries. Not only was the weather hot and the flies out, so Blueberry was shaking his head all over the place, when I rode in I saw it was Peter Storr and Christian Landolt, another respected judge and rider, judging. They were both sat at C, so I was going to have to do the halt-rein back right slap-bang in front of them.

I rode down the centre line, halted, went to rein back … and Blueberry did not move. He was locked in my hand, absolutely rigid. I tried to pull him backwards but he was like a rock, his hooves were rooted to the spot. The only part of him that was moving was his head, and eventually it got to the point where he'd turned it so much I could see his face. The look he was giving me just said: 'What are you *doing*?' I tried and tried to get him to move, and eventually Peter, who was chuckling away, stage-whispered across: 'PULL HARDER!' I was mortified but it obviously wasn't going to happen, so I just had to give up, put it behind me and get on with the rest of the test. In the end we finished second which, fortunately, was still enough to qualify us for the Five-Year-Old Shearwater Championship at the Nationals in September. Getting Blueberry out to more shows was obviously going to be crucial for both of us, but it always used to amaze me that Carl would just ship me off on my own with his horse. He would arrange for his occasional driver, Ian Newman, to collect us and then he would just wish us luck and wave us all off in his little three-and-a-half tonne van.

Ian was the loveliest man but he also liked to talk, and the whole journey he'd be telling me about his work or the weather and I'd be going crazy because I needed to be reading my test. I was grooming for myself, too, and soon realised I couldn't do it all on my own. Luckily, there was still someone I could call on for back-up.

My relationship with my mum had improved since we'd had some time apart: she'd begun to understand dressage was different from showing, and that when I was competing I needed to make my plan, stick to it and not be distracted. She drove me, Blueberry and Dez to the Nationals that year and it ended up being a real family outing as my dad and Dean came too. We all travelled up to Stoneleigh together, and at night Mum and Dad slept in the live-in part of the lorry and Dean and I put some carpet down in the back and camped out. I loved staying in the lorry again and having our barbecues in the evening – my dad was always an amazing barbecue cook. We'd put the awning up on the side of the lorry and sit outside eating and talking with friends, reminiscing about the old times. The feeling of having both my parents there to watch me after a year when it felt like we'd been living such separate lives was really special.

I was so excited to be going out on Blueberry in front of everybody at Stoneleigh and didn't want to let them down. Fortunately the weather was quite cold – no flies, so I was delighted – and Blueberry was really, really good. We came away with two titles, the Novice and the Five-Year-Old Championship, and I felt so happy that I had proved to Carl I could deliver on him. I was also leading all the way on Dez in the Advanced Medium, until Carl came in on TMovistar and bumped us into second place.

Being in Carl's presence, at his yard and riding his horses, was still something I had to pinch myself to believe, and I could never have afforded to pay for the training and opportunities I was getting with him. All Dez's livery costs were paid too, so I certainly didn't expect any extra cash in hand, but I also had to survive and I literally had no money.

The upshot was that I had to be working as many hours as there were in a day trying to make ends meet, and sometimes I'd be so broke I couldn't even drive home to see Mum because I couldn't afford to put fuel in the car.

* * *

In 2008, Dean and I moved in together, renting a flat that had been recently converted from stables at Sandra Biddlecombe's yard. It was a lovely, cosy place, but at night-time you could hear every single sound: the horses banging their head collars or kicking their doors or chewing their feed buckets. Sometimes one of them would start and you'd think it had got cast and stuck in their stall, so you'd get up to go and look and of course it would just be playing with its bucket or digging the floor up. I'd never know whether to be relieved or infuriated because it would mean yet another night when I hadn't slept properly, and my days were long and tiring enough already.

After I'd finished at Carl's each afternoon, I'd go and ride for either Sandra or Kate Carter, another friend of Carl's, to try and get some cash. Up until now, Dean had been working in his dad's pub, but when he began a new job at a hotel in Corse Lawn there'd be times when we hardly saw each other. Dean usually worked the night shift and at weekends, and because my week-ends were spent either at shows or riding or teaching, he'd often be coming in the door as I was going out.

It was stressful for both of us, and I'd ring Mum at night sometimes in tears because I didn't know if I could do it any more. A lot of the horses I was riding were just being broken, and because they were young and naughty I'd end up getting bucked off. Mum would tell me not to do it because I couldn't afford to get hurt, but the way I saw it, I couldn't afford to turn work down. I had to live somehow, and even though it was tough I still thought it was all good experience: even with the young, naughty ones you can still learn things.

Sometimes we'd have to ring up Dean's stepmum or my mum to do an online shop for us because we couldn't afford it ourselves, and Sandra also ended up being like a second mum. Until then, I'd been happy living with Lucy, so moving to another new place was quite daunting for me. When I'd taken over the ride on Blueberry, Lucy had been upset and I knew it, although because I felt bad about it I was a bit scared ever to bring it into the open and say anything. We'd stayed good friends, though, and kept in touch even after she left Carl's in 2009 to set up on her own.

Sandra, on the other hand, was someone I hardly knew at the time, but it wasn't long before she'd started to come knocking on my door in the evening with casseroles or cakes or apple pies. She made the best fish pie, which I absolutely love, and if she was making dinner for her family or had guests coming over, she'd always make extra of whatever they were having and give it to me. Tony, Sandra's husband, was great too, and they were both a huge source of support.

Another bonus of being at Sandra's was that I could have my Boxer, Winnie, come to live with me. Winnie had been a twenty-first birthday present and Mum had been looking after her, but when I got her back to Gloucestershire she showed she didn't think much of being left alone by shredding all my coats to pieces. It wasn't long before she started coming with me to the yard, and when Mum bred a litter of toy poodle crosses I got her a friend, Hugo, who was the smallest of the litter and too irresistible not to have.

I've still got Winnie and Hugo today, as well as Harley (another poodle) and Jingles, my rescued golden retriever. They all come along to the yard, and it never ceases to amaze me how they know the exact second I've finished schooling and am ready for a gallop in the fields. I always think it does the horses good for them to be around, because it gets them used to quick movements and makes them less spooky, although I have to say Blueberry has never taken the slightest interest in them unless they go near his food, in which case his ears go flat back.

The year 2008 had got off to a good start with the Winter Championships at Addington. Blueberry won the Elementary Champion, but pulling it out of the bag to win the Advanced Medium on Dez, my own horse, was really special. Dez had spent a lot of his career being second and marked down in young horse classes, and the following week the two of us had a big picture in *Horse & Hound*. I'd had pictures in there before in my showing days, but this was the first time I'd been recognised for dressage, and the reporter wrote that the crowd had been 'stunned by my fluent performance'. It really did feel like things were taking off, but I had no idea how much until, out of the blue, I got an invitation to the Beijing Olympics.

The Olympic Ambition Programme is one of the ways the British Olympic Association tries to develop British chances of medal success. Because the atmosphere of an Olympics is so unlike any other competition, the Ambition Programme is intended to give potential Olympic athletes a preview in order to inspire them and help them and their coaches prepare.

Based on my record with Fernandez, Caroline Griffiths had nominated me to the Equestrian Performance Manager, who had put me forward for consideration by the BOA. I'd been successful, so was now being invited to join the Ambition Programme and fly out for five days in August to watch the best athletes in the world.

When I put the phone down I was honestly so excited I didn't know whether I was laughing or crying. Dean was jumping up and down, and when I ran next door to tell Sandra she cracked open the champagne right there. Tony had been in the shower when I arrived and soon joined us, although when he went to hug me he accidentally dropped his towel and flashed me, which is a sight I'll never forget.

Daryl Thickitt (who now coaches the British dressage pony team) and Sarah Millis had also been chosen to fly out, and Jane Bartle-Wilson came as our coach. Jane had been the Chef d'Equipe for the British team between 1993 and 2000, and had ridden at the Los Angeles Olympics in 1984 on her horse Pinocchio. Because she'd competed at an Olympics herself she was able to give us lots of interesting inside information, and she had such energy that she was great at making us all feel motivated. I didn't know Sarah that well, but Daryl, like Jane, was also very outward-going and as amazed as I was at what was happening to him. One of our best off-duty trips together was to a warehouse absolutely filled with dodgy goods: you name it, they'd got the fake. My dad had always taught me to barter whenever we visited markets in Portugal – as I knew all too well, if you don't ask, you don't get – and I don't know how much I ended up saving the others, who were ready to fork out full price for everything.

Part of the idea of the Ambition Programme is that you got a sense of what goes on behind the scenes and experience other sports besides your own. We were given a tour of the Olympic Village and the British training camp, and we were also taken to watch a tennis match, although who was playing I couldn't tell you now. I'd never watched tennis before, didn't know the rules, and really struggled to sit there with my head just going left and right, left and right, for hours on end. It was incredibly humid, too, which is one of the things I remember most about watching day one of the Grand Prix at the Hong Kong Sports Institute. The seats were plastic so you kept sticking to them and you could feel the heat pumping off the people sitting next to you. God only knows how the riders in all their gear managed, and it wasn't a surprise to hear that Laura Bechtolsheimer, who was riding Mistral Højris (Alf), had fainted with heat exhaustion after her test.

The British team of Laura, Emma Hindle and Jane Gregory finished fifth over all behind Germany, the Netherlands, Denmark and Sweden. Emma also finished seventh in the individual competition but, ironically, although I had made it to Beijing, Carl hadn't – both his top horses, Dolendo and Lecantos, had gone lame earlier in the summer.

Carl is not the kind of person who, when bad things happen, sits in the corner crying, although if it had been me, that's probably what I would have done. He was disappointed, obviously, but he knew horses go wrong sometimes and that you've just got to carry on. Watching how he dealt with it felt like another big lesson, but it's true that you never really know how these things feel until they happen to you.

Not long after I'd been back from Beijing, Dez came in from the field with an injury. He was probably only a tenth lame but I knew he wasn't right, although none of the vets I had come to look at him knew what the problem was. He must have pulled or jarred something and so we were advised to put him on box rest, but as he wasn't now being competed, I had to move him out of Carl's yard to free up his box for a livery. There was plenty of space at Sandra's so that wasn't a problem, but it was while he was there that disaster struck: Dez somehow managed to pull the bolt of his stable door across with his teeth and let himself out. Because he'd been cooped up he went absolutely crazy, and by the time we managed to catch him, it was too late: this time he was totally lame.

The first vet to see Dez thought he had torn the meniscus in his stifle, which is a career-ending injury. The next vet to look at him wrote him off too, and we were told the best thing we could do for him was to turn him away to grass for the rest of his life or put him to sleep. I was so desperate I even tried a third vet, but the verdict was the same: Dez might not ever come back into work, and he'd definitely never be sound enough to compete at Grand Prix.

It was horrendous. I had such a good partnership with that little horse and he had a heart of gold: you could have ridden him round a test in just a headcollar and rope if you'd wanted. He was the horse Mum and I had bought and I'd trained up to the brink of what seemed like it was going to be a brilliant career, and now we were being told he was never going to come right.

Although Dez was insured, I had to pay his livery costs at Sandra's, and as time went on and his vets' bills still kept coming, we surpassed his insurance limit. Every penny I had was going into him, and what made it worse was that, just before he'd been injured, Mum and I had been offered a very substantial amount of money for him. We'd decided to turn it down because Mum was adamant that Dez was meant for me as my 2012 horse, but now I had no horse and no money.

There comes a point where you have to draw a line and I think, had it not been for Mum, I would have given up. But my Mum is stubborn: it's where I get it from. One day she was at Sandra's yard when another vet, Kieran Patterson, also happened to be there and

Mum, being the kind of person who speaks to everyone, began to tell Kieran about Dez.

Kieran advised us to try a specialist called Sven Kold, who thought that the damage to Dez's stifle was less severe than we'd first been led to believe. Sven operated on Dez and within two or three weeks you could see a dramatic improvement. But he would still need months of rehab and that was time I just didn't have: I'd been getting up even earlier to hand walk him before mucking him out and going to work, and was nearly exhausted. So Mum decided to take Dez back to a livery yard near her house and nurse him herself.

When it comes to getting animals sound, Mum is like a magician: she's even managed to heal Winnie when she's been lame. She wasn't going to be defeated this time and anything that could be done to get Dez sound, she did, including taking him for hydrotherapy on a water treadmill.

It was all costing us thousands of pounds, and I decided then that if I was ever offered life-changing money for a horse again, I'd take it. It might sound shocking but, much as I love all of my horses, if the right offer with the right home comes along, they're all for sale. Our is a sport that costs so much when you're at the top, and I never wanted to be in the position of having nothing again – and, hard as it is selling horses, it's often the only way you can keep competing.

The other person I owe thanks for her help with Dez's rehab is Jayne Turney. As Dez began to get better, Jayne started hacking him out, then slowly reintroducing him to trotting and cantering. Every month we could increase his workload a bit more, and I was so grateful to Jayne as I knew she was utterly trustworthy and would never get carried away. It's very easy when you've got a horse that's been off to overdo it, but Jayne understood that if Dez was meant to have five minutes of trot, he had five minutes and no more.

I went home to Mum's for Christmas, and on Christmas day my sister, my Dad and I all went up to visit Dez. It was snowing, so it felt special already, and for the first time in a year I was able to sit on his back. It felt so good to be on him again after thinking it would never happen, but he still had many more months of recovery ahead and wouldn't compete again until 2011.

7

Fun and Games

AFTER DEZ WAS injured, I felt like it was game over for me for London 2012. I still had Blueberry, but I didn't know for how long: although Carl had decided to keep him, he was now thinking of taking the ride on him back.

With each year Blueberry's headshaking had got a bit less and he was winning more and more. As a Group 1 rider Carl wasn't able to compete at Elementary and Novice level, but once Blueberry got to Prix St. Georges, which would probably be in another year, the plan became that he would take over from there.

On the one hand, I felt so lucky to have had even the time I'd had with Blueberry: even if I had to let Carl have him back, I'd learned so much and had such great opportunities. But I also genuinely felt like I'd found my partner, and that if I kept winning, and kept working to make myself a better rider and Blueberry a better horse, Carl would see the partnership we'd developed and allow us to carry on. At the end of the day I knew all I could do was try, and so every opportunity and every chance I got, I took it.

At around this time, Carl sold a part share in Blueberry to Roly Luard, with whom he'd owned other horses and who had also seen Blueberry's potential. Meanwhile, he and I carried on clocking up the titles: the Shearwater Six-Year-Old Champion, Elementary and Medium Champion at the 2008 Nationals, and the Advanced Medium Champion at the Winter

Championships in April 2009. While I was there I also picked up the Elementary Champion on Duchess IV, who belonged to the owners of another of Carl's horses. It wasn't an experience I really enjoyed: she was a beautiful mare, but as lazy as sin. Blueberry was the kind of horse you had to work at making calmer, but Duchess had absolutely no motivation and getting her round that test I really felt like I was pushing a baby out.

As ever, I looked on it as good experience. I was out every other weekend on one horse or another – riding for cash and to help clients out – and all the time my aim was to better myself as a rider and make Carl proud of the way I was learning and developing. If he gave me an exercise to do, I'd go away and work on it and make sure I'd improved by the next time. I couldn't think of anything worse for him than having to tell me the same things over and over again.

One of the things I was still struggling with was my sitting trot, which made me rely too much on my hands for balance. Carl would often tell me that showing had given me bad hands, which was true, and because he's the kind of person who gives everyone a nickname I ended up as Edwina Scissorhands, or Eddie.

The key was getting stronger in my core, but even though I was swimming I still wasn't fit enough, plus I was about two stone heavier than I should have been. Staying in shape is something I've always had to work at quite hard, but when I'd been at Judy's, Jayne and I would get through a loaf of bread with butter and jam for lunch every day. We'd wash it down with tea and biscuits, and owners would always bring cakes and treats when they came to the yard. I look back now and think it's no wonder I was the size of the house, but I only realised it was a problem when I heard on the grapevine that Carl thought I could do with losing some weight.

Hearing that broke my heart, but he was right. I didn't want to be anorexic, but if I wasn't fit I couldn't do my job so I decided then that I was going to start going to the gym and get myself a personal trainer.

Unlike the first couple of PTs I tried, Jo Theyer understood that I still needed to be able to walk and sit down when she'd finished with me. She also came to study me ride and helped me identify that my right leg was weaker then my left. If you're weak on one side it's obvious that your horse will have problems on that side too, and it seems ridiculous that we spend heaps of money paying for our horses to have physio and massages but don't think about the problems we might be causing as riders.

Opening people's eyes to the importance of rider fitness was something that I think I achieved, particularly after the London Olympics, when I'd often be asked about it. But although I was taking my health and physical performance more seriously I didn't gave my safety a thought until it was almost too late.

I'd never ridden in a helmet at home, and at shows I wore my top hat like everybody else. Then one day the horse I was schooling bucked me off and my head hit the boards at the side of the arena. When I woke up I couldn't remember a thing: my mind was blank. I wasn't aware of being in pain, but I was crying with panic because I couldn't remember what had happened, why I was on the floor or even what day it was.

I was rushed by ambulance to hospital in Gloucester while Carl phoned Dean with the news, a call Dean had always said he dreaded getting. My mum and sister drove up from home as fast as they could and sat with me in A&E, but the worst moment was when I felt blood beginning to trickle out of my ear. I truly believed I was having a brain haemorrhage and was about to die, although the blood turned out to be from a burst eardrum. However, an MRI showed that I had a small skull fracture, which meant I was strictly forbidden from riding for at least three weeks.

Unfortunately I had my regionals coming up fast. I promised the doctors that I'd be sensible but a few days later I was back riding again, trying to ignore the fact that I had such a headache and my skull felt like it was full of jelly.

I started wearing a crash hat at home straight afterwards, although I didn't compete in one for the first time until 2012. Looking back now, when crash hats are the norm and it's seeing people in top hats that looks weird, the uproar it caused seems unbelievable. Some people felt that I wasn't respecting the traditions of the sport and I think some even thought it was a publicity stunt, but I saw it as just taking care of myself: it seemed pretty darn stupid to me to put image over looking after your head.

Carl's nickname for Blueberry was 'The Professor' because he always said it was as though he'd read the dressage encyclopedia in his stable. He had trainability, but he was also naturally talented in that he had the ability to sit – which is essential for exercises like piaffe and pirouettes – and he could push when you asked for extensions. Most horses are better at one or the other, but Blueberry could do both without stressing himself out, although that doesn't mean he found everything easy. You'd never have imagined that Valegro once found it hard to piaffe, but to start with he was so hot he couldn't find the rhythm. Sometimes, when you're training a young horse to piaffe, you lightly touch a whip on top of its bum to encourage it to find the bounce, but if you did that with Blueberry he was so sensitive and willing to go he'd just try to canter.

He didn't quite know what to do with all the power he had, which also caused me problems trying to teach him flying changes. Flying changes were easy for Blueberry, you just put your leg on and he was off like a rocket: it was like an explosion across the diagonal. The problem was he'd then get so excited and strong he'd start trying to do them everywhere. I had to keep doing a single change, patting him, then bringing him back to walk, over and over, so he learned that sometimes one was all I wanted. When he'd understood that, I could start putting them together, and his one-time changes ended up being like nothing I'd ever sat on in my entire life: you felt like he was climbing a hill and just getting higher and higher and higher with every stride.

With passage, his huge engine again caused difficulties. Blueberry's hind legs were so good that all their power pushed him forward and then he couldn't quite cope with lifting his front end up as well. Because he was still a young horse he hadn't yet developed the ability to balance himself, so every time I tried to create a bit of lift he pulled more and more on my arms. Some horses are born with really nice mouths and are very light in your hands, and some have harder mouths and take a strong hold. Then there are horses like Blueberry who have mouths like bricks and by the time we'd finished my arms would be absolutely burning.

As I began to ride Blueberry at bigger shows, Carl would try to ensure he was there to warm us up. I'd had it drilled into me by Judy not to rely on anyone, and although Carl's advice was always helpful, what I most appreciated was simply having him there to give me a pat on the leg and a few words of encouragement, usually just to go in and enjoy it. Now, though, we were getting to the point where instead of just being my coach and Blueberry's owner, Carl was also someone I had to beat.

The first time we competed against each other was in a World Class-sponsored Prix St Georges class at the Royal Windsor Horse Show in May 2009. It was a special competition for young horses with international potential and Valegro was the youngest taking part, a year younger than Carl's eight-year-old Uthopia.

Any competition I enter I want to win, so obviously I wanted to beat Carl, but I never thought I actually would. Uti was a really powerful, bouncy little machine, plus he had Carl on his back, so I decided I was just going to go in and have fun being on Blueberry. When I came out I had the feeling that it had gone all right, and my sister, who had driven me down, said it looked good, but realising that I'd actually beaten Carl and Uti into second was surreal. I felt so chuffed and proud of myself, but it was quite strange in the prize-giving. All I could think was, 'Oh my God, *Carl* is behind *me!*' I didn't want to look over at him because I honestly felt a bit sheepish, although of course in the car on the way home with Emma-Jayne I was whooping and cheering my head off.

Carl and I both knew that Blueberry and Uti were very talented horses, but at that stage in their careers you couldn't have said that either of them was definitely going to be an Olympic gold medal winner. A horse can be brilliant in the school at home, but if it doesn't want to perform, you can't make it. Having a horse that wants to work with you is crucial, which is why the partnership between horse and rider is so important.

One combination that was then starting to stand out above everybody else's was the Dutch rider Edward Gal and Totilas, who was a picture-perfect black stallion. Totilas was two years older than Blueberry, and in 2009 he was just at the start of his record-breaking career.

I remember seeing them first in the kur (a dressage test ridden to music) at the European Championships at Windsor, which was where Totilas became the first horse ever to score over 90 per cent. It was the kind of performance that gives you goosebumps: the arena was floodlit and you could see Windsor Castle lit up against the night sky in the background. There was a sell-out crowd of 8,000 and when Edward raised his hat at the end there was a standing ovation that went on for about five minutes.

Edward always manages to have total control over his horses, which makes him a fascinating rider to watch, and Totilas you just couldn't look away from. He had incredible presence, and in his extended trot and piaffe/passage his legs would nearly touch his nose they came so high. I hadn't seen a horse move like that before – it was spectacular. I would have loved to have had a sit on him because you never know what a horse is going to be like until you do: sometimes it can feel completely different when you're actually on its back to how you'd imagined. Totilas, though, I'm sure would have felt as incredible as he looked. He was without doubt a superstar and for many people he and Edward were the ones really to put dressage on the map.

Totilas would be the horse Valegro was always compared to, and as it became obvious just how good Blueberry was people started to wonder why I was riding him when Carl had his pick of the horses. I knew people were already intrigued by me and wanted to know why Carl had taken me on, so I did feel like I had something to prove.

* * *

Going in to the Advanced Medium at the Nationals in 2009, Blueberry had a clean sweep of titles. This would be the only one we didn't win, and it was the only time I ever let my nerves and mental state get the better of me. I felt that I'd got so far and come through so much with him – his head shaking, Carl wanting to sell him – that if this really was going to be our last competition together before Carl took him back for Prix St Georges it needed to be the best I could possibly make it. But right from the start, things went wrong.

Because Blueberry had so much energy, the routine I'd developed was to ride him twice at shows. I'd get him out in the morning, give him a little trot and canter for twenty minutes, put him away, then get him out again to do my forty-minute warm-up. This time we'd been drawn so early that the arenas weren't open when I wanted to be getting on him for the first time, so when I went to warm him up, he was electric.

There's a vibe at the National Championships that can make even an experienced horse on edge: it can be terrible weather, there are flags and marquees snapping and flapping and horses and people walking everywhere. Valegro was so fresh, and I wanted to win our last test so badly, that when I went to do the serpentine he absolutely exploded in one of the changes. It was just enough to drop me to second behind Michael Eilberg on Dornroschen, Michael having recently switched to dressage from showjumping.

I was so disappointed, and made up my mind then that whatever happened, I wasn't going to put myself under such pressure to win that I actually stopped loving being out there. But was I was ever going to get that chance with Blueberry again? I felt gutted that my career with him might be about to end, and to end this way.

OK, coming second wasn't a disaster, but we'd won pretty much every time out until now.

We went home, and after that I tried to take each day as it came. As ever with Carl there was never any discussion about the future, so I had no clue what he was thinking as 2009 came to a close. Then in January I found myself back out on Blueberry at another show. So was this going to be my last ride? I still hadn't got any idea. But as time went on, show followed show followed show and we kept on winning and winning.

There was never a moment when I realised Carl wasn't actually going to take Blueberry back. Nothing was said, and if we hadn't been doing so well, I don't think Carl would have hesitated to take the ride. But he himself was notching up the wins with Uti, and having been given so many opportunities by his mentor, Dr Bechtolsheimer, I knew Carl felt he wanted to give someone else a turn. What I didn't know then was the other reason he finally decided to let me and Blueberry carry on: the idea he'd had that he and I on Uti and Blueberry might make the basis of a British team. Of course in all our wildest dreams neither of us could have foreseen how that was going to work out.

Uncertainty isn't something I'm good at, and it had felt like I'd been through a lot of it lately. So when Dean started acting suspiciously just before Christmas, I got more than usually stressed. I can read Dean like a book – I look at his face and I know exactly when he's up to something – so I wasn't about to let it go. 'What are you up to? Come on, what's going on?' I found out when I got into bed one night and discovered a diamond ring between the sheets: Dean had been planning a more romantic proposal, but I was getting so suspicious he'd decided he'd better get it done and dusted before he seriously cheesed me off.

Having fallen for him at first sight, I obviously said yes, although I think my mum was a bit surprised. I'd never been one for getting loved up when I was younger because I was always so much more interested in my ponies, and I don't think she had me down as the marrying sort. But with Dean I'd never had any doubt. I didn't feel like I wanted to set a date straight away – I'm not *that* much of a romantic – but it did feel like the start of our future together.

In the New Year, Dean and I moved from Sandra Biddlecombe's flat to a little cottage in the grounds of Carl's new yard. Oaklebrook Mill is a sixteenth-century millhouse set in thirty acres of land, and Carl had set about transforming it using the best ideas from other yards he'd seen. Our horses' well-being is at the centre of everything we do, so most of the stables have views in two directions to make sure the horses have lots of fresh air and things to keep them interested. We also have our solarium and wash bays at the side of our indoor school, away from the stable block, so that the horses' work is separate from where they relax and chill out.

It's a place that always has a lovely atmosphere, although you get there sometimes and it feels as though you're walking into a zoo. Carl loves his birds, so as well as his dogs, my dogs and a couple of cats, we have guinea fowl, peacocks, parrots, doves and chickens. There's usually something dashing in front of your horse or sitting on the mirrors in the indoor school squawking, and the guinea fowl make such a goddamn noise that when I was living on-site I swear it nearly drove me crazy. They had so much land to go round, and yet they still ended up sitting right outside our cottage. Sometimes I think our horses must get to a show and breathe a sigh of relief just to have some peace and quiet for a while.

Our yard's horse walker is a special design that Carl had imported from New Zealand on the recommendation of the event rider Mark Todd. Carl had evented early in his career and had previously helped Mark with his dressage, but when Mark needed some help in late 2009, Carl was busy and put Mark in touch with me.

Dressage is like any other sport in that it changes over time. Trish Gardiner, who hacks Blueberry out when I'm not schooling him, rode on the British dressage team between 1977 and 1991 and at the Seoul Olympics in 1988. She got out her pictures to show me recently and it was like another era: how they used to ride in those saddles I have no idea. They were probably top of the range in those days, but it made me realise the luxury we have today because they looked like flat pieces of leather to me.

We have much more equipment than any riders before us ever had and our style of riding is different too, which is what I had to get across to Mark. He rode at (and won) his first Badminton in 1980 and competed in his first Olympics in 1984, but when I started teaching him I had to break it to him that things had moved on since then.

'Mark, is that horse on the bit? Is that what it's meant to look like?'

'What's wrong with it?'

'Well, you've got to shorten up your reins by about ten inches for a start ...'

Back in the day, dressage didn't much affect the final result of a three-day event, but now you can't get away with a horse that's behind your leg and stiff as a plank of wood. I'd always imagined event horses to be sharp, supple and forward-thinking because of all the galloping they have to do, but it wasn't until I began riding Mark's that I realised I was going to have my work cut out.

At the time, he was riding a horse called Grass Valley (Riley), who would go on to win team bronze with Mark at the 2010 World Equestrian Games. Riley, bless him, was such a lovely horse, but dressage wasn't the easiest phase for him and like many event horses, flying changes were something he really struggled to do. When you're jumping and cantering across country you can change leg off any old stride, but in the dressage arena you've got to get a clean change when you ask for it.

Sometimes we'd get halfway through a lesson and Mark would start pretending to be exasperated and telling me to do it myself if it was all so easy.

'It's no good me doing it, Mark, I know how to do it. *You're* the one who's got to do it.'

To this day people are amazed that I'd stand and shout at seven-time Olympian Sir Mark Todd. 'Do you honestly tell him what to do?' 'Well, of course I tell him what to do! He's not paying me to sit there and tell him how wonderful he is!' But being asked to help him was a huge honour, especially because I was still quite new to dressage myself. Like Carl, Mark had been a real idol to me, and as my career developed he was always ready to give me advice on how to deal with things. In May 2017, at the age of sixty-one, he finished with two horses in the top five at Badminton, which proves again what a genius he is. He's a lovely guy and someone I hope will always be in my life.

By March 2010 Blueberry and I were ready to make our international and small tour debut on the Sunshine Tour in Spain. It was a fantastic start: we came away with wins in six out of our seven tests and finished second in the seventh. It was the first time that any judges outside England had seen Valegro, and I think he turned a lot of people's heads.

Carl had bought Uti out and they won all of their classes, two Grand Prix and two Specials, but Carl let me have the ride on another of his horses, Don Archie, in the Six-Year-Old Championship.

Going from Blueberry, who was perfect, to Archie, was quite a shock: he was a really good mover and had a lovely canter but when Carl first bought him he'd had to sign a disclaimer because Archie had already put so many people on the floor.

Carl had initially got his friend, the event rider Greg Smith, to be a test pilot, because Greg is great with young, green horses. But when Greg went home to New Zealand, Carl decided it was going to be my job to teach Archie how to trot.

Carl was starting to admit that trot was one of the very few things I was better at than he was. Archie, however, was what you might call quite opinionated, and a lot of those early months were spent being jumped out of the arena or just galloped off with. I loved him, but most of what I was trying to do with him – making him bend and be supple, lateral work – he really did not like.

The warm-up arena at the Sunshine Tour is huge, and one day I was training Archie in it when he stuck his head in the air and decided to bolt. We went round and round and then into a hedge, and when I looked back at Carl he was standing with a friend, watching and laughing. Well, I'm very glad it was funny for someone, I thought. I finally managed to get Archie out of the leaves and we rode back to the arena, where the Spanish team trainer Jan Bemelmans had seen what happened. 'I think you need a double-bridle,' he said. 'Yes,' I said, with feeling, 'I think I do.'

Having some brakes helped, although Archie would still bolt every time I asked for a flying change. I know

Carl was nervous for us when we went in to the final, but I touched wood and Archie turned out to be as good as gold: we came out with 79 per cent which was more than enough for first place.

It was a new experience for me to be on the international scene and travelling abroad with Carl. We flew out to Spain together and Carl checked into a rented apartment as he normally does, but I'd planned to sleep in the lorry. I soon found I was getting lonely and one night I rang Mum and asked if she could fly out. We ended up renting a gorgeous villa in Vejer de la Frontera, and later the Dockleys came out for a holiday as well. In the evenings Mum and I would cook at home or walk into town for dinner at one of the little tapas bars, and even though the weather was filthy we had a lovely time. One day when I'd got completely soaked Mum decided she was going to wash a load of my breeches: she still loves all that side of things and is usually an expert at getting breeches white. This time, however, she decided she was going to dry them on the radiator. Need I say that when we came down in the morning we found my breeches were now nice and white and crisply burned all across the seams.

Back at home there was another new ride: Supanova, a dark bay Hanoverian who we all called Neville. Like Valegro, Supanova was owned by Carl and Roly Luard; unlike Blueberry, Neville was probably one of the ugliest horses we'd ever had on the yard. He was a good 16.3 hands and had an incredibly powerful hind end, but a really skinny neck and a head that was never going to win any prizes for beauty. He was a very rude horse to handle, too, and had his own opinion on life: he wouldn't want to go on the lorry, wouldn't want to leave the other horses, and made himself quite difficult for the girls to handle. But he was showing signs of being super-talented at piaffe and passage, and although we only had a handful of outings, we won several times at Advanced Medium. Spencer Wilton eventually took over the ride in 2012, and four years later they were beginning on their own fairytale journey when they were selected for the Rio Olympics.

Carl is someone around whom there is never a dull moment, and the fun and games continued when a TV crew from Horse & Country arrived to film the mini-series *At Home with Carl Hester*. Carl's dad is the actor Anthony Smee and in his twenties Carl modelled for *GQ* magazine, so performing in front of a camera is something he was born to do. Put a mic in front of Carl and he can talk for hours and hours; Horse & Country had already filmed a couple of his 'Fantastic Elastic' master classes, one of which featured me on a six-year-old Blueberry. I, on the otherhand, absolutely detested that side of things. The idea of a film crew following me around and filming everything made me incredibly uncomfortable, but by the time Carl had finished telling me how he did things in his day, and how I had to pose with my chin up and tongue to the roof of my mouth, I ended up forgetting they were there because I was laughing so much.

The crew came with us to the 2010 Nationals, where I ended up losing a bet with the *Horse & Hound* photographer, Kevin Sparrow. I love browsing the trade stands at shows, and Kevin had managed to catch me admiring a range of hot tubs. They looked quite luxurious, bubbling away, and Kevin wanted a picture then and there, but I said he'd have to wait. I was about to ride Blueberry in the Prix St Georges and I promised Kevin that if we won, I'd not only let him have his picture, I'd jump into the hot tub fully clothed. Of course, I never seriously thought I was going to have to do it, and when I came out of my test I was moaning away: Blueberry had been hot and strong, so I couldn't really get my legs on him, which meant the test was underpowered. Then we got 72.05 per cent, 0.16 of a per cent more than Gareth Hughes. Kevin won his bet, and I ended up climbing into a hot tub with a glass of champagne and all my whites on, being photographed by Kevin *and* filmed for TV.

As I was now a Group 1 Rider myself, I couldn't compete at the lower levels. The previous year, I'd bought a horse with Dean and the Dockleys, Frederico (Chico), who I was hoping to train up and sell on. I got Katie Bailey, one of Carl's grooms, to compete him for me at the Nationals and both of them did well in the Novice Open. Spectating was quite a weird experience, though: I felt like I rode Katie's whole test with her. I'm sure anyone watching me would have thought I was just like one of those nervous showjumping mothers whose legs fly up in the air every time their son or daughter goes over a fence.

It was while we were filming with Horse & Country that Carl went on record as saying that the aim for Blueberry was London 2012. I was also asked what my plans were for the future, to which I replied that I'd quite like to get to the Olympics and win a medal so I could put it on my wall and retire.

At that point it really did feel like life couldn't get much better. I was engaged to Dean, I was competing on Blueberry, and Dez was also starting to come back into work. But the next step was the big one, and the one I'd been working towards from the beginning: the step up to Grand Prix.

8

Record Breakers

QUESTIONS HAD BEEN asked before about why I and not Carl was riding Valegro: it had happened ahead of the Advanced Medium at the 2009 Nationals, which had added to the pressure that day. I'd been able to put it to the back of my mind before, but when it happened again at the start of 2011 the negative comments went deeper. It really dented my confidence and made me doubt myself. Maybe I wasn't good enough to be riding Carl's horse. Then I realised I basically had two choices: I could either let the negativity get to me and fall to pieces, or I could turn it around. 'Right,' I thought, 'you're not going to defeat me. I'm going to go out there and I'm going to show you what I can do.'

Blueberry and I made our Grand Prix debut at Addington on 22 January. At only nine he was still very green, and his one-time changes were so big that I could barely fit all fifteen of them on the diagonal. At home I'd make mistake after mistake after mistake: I'd get them, then I'd lose them, then I'd get them, then I'd lose them – I got to the point of thinking I was never going to get it right.

In Zwolle a few weeks earlier we'd come second in the Prix St Georges to Edward Gal and Voice, and third in the Intermediate 1 Music. But at Addington we not only won with 74.62 per cent, we also carried off our changes – for me, almost more of a highlight than the

115

three tens Blueberry was awarded for his extended trots and canters.

The months after that felt like some of the most incredible of my entire career. Carl had taken responsibility for planning my competition schedule so Blueberry and I weren't just dropped in at the deep end. He wanted to get me used to competing at the top level without too much pressure. That meant the next stop was Vidauban in the South of France and to go there, win two Grand Prix and two Specials and score between 73 and 74 per cent every time, felt unreal.

I was still having problems with my changes, but even though I had a few frustrating errors in the first of the Specials at Vidauban a couple of judges awarded us upwards of 76 per cent. 'Holy moly,' I thought, 'if I can get scores like that even with mistakes, imagine what I can get without!' And these were international judges, too, which was a rebuff to the people who'd thought my mark at Addington was too high and not deserved.

But I didn't want to get carried away. After I'd ridden I sat on the sidelines trying to watch, watch, watch, absorbing all the different techniques and learning as much as I could about all the different things the other riders were doing.

Judy Harvey was also at Vidauban with her horse Fitzcerraldo, and we sat together and she talked things through with me while I tried to pick up all the information I could. The fact that I'd beaten her barely crossed my mind. I was proud, obviously, but when I'm competing I just try and focus on my own riding. People were already starting to talk about Blueberry and I didn't want the pressure of that to affect my performance, so I tried as much as possible to carry on in my own little zone.

One thing Carl and I had realised after Addington was that Blueberry needed to know the lines of the Grand Prix test. With some horses, especially later in their careers, you wish they'd forget where they're going because they're anticipating and trying to take over. Blueberry and I were so new to it all we needed familiarity, and having wobbled our way round Addington, hoping and praying it was going to happen, we were already more confident in what we were doing at Vidauban.

While I was focusing on Blueberry, Carl was already thinking ahead to the European Championships in Rotterdam in August. Blueberry and Uthopia were near certainties for the team, but Carl wanted to qualify Dez as a reserve horse in case either he or I had a problem.

I knew how much Carl loved Dezzie and when he had suggested that he ride him at Zwolle in what would be his first Grand Prix, it was a pleasure for me to say yes. My mum was disappointed it wasn't me on Dez on his Grand Prix debut, but he tried his heart out for Carl to finish third and they also came back with a second in the Freestyle. Then the pair of them finished second to me and Blueberry in the Grand Prix at Addington in January: in fact, there was just 0.36 per cent between us. My turn with Dez came at Addington in April, where we finished second to Laura Bechtolsheimer in both the Grand Prix and Freestyle. It was such a proud moment knowing that I'd been the one who'd trained him up to that level, although riding a Grand Prix on Dez felt a bit strange after Blueberry. Dez wasn't able to cover the ground in the same way, but because I wasn't having to work all the time just to contain his power, the same job felt much easier.

In April, Carl and I took Uthopia and Blueberry to Saumur in France, and that's where (according to Carl) the rivalry between us really started. We came away with a win and a second place each: Carl beat me on Uthopia in the Grand Prix with 74 per cent, and then Blueberry and I won the Special. I know Carl felt he deserved to win that, too – there was only 0.08 per cent between us, although it would have been more if I'd hadn't made an error. I came out feeling frustrated I'd let Blueberry down, but I was starting to find beating Carl a bit addictive. The first time it had happened had seemed like a fluke and I'd actually felt a bit embarrassed for myself, but the more it happened, the more I was starting to love it.

I'd always wanted to win, but one of the things Carl helped teach me was how to ride a test competitively. When you have to learn a test, it's not about just riding the movements and remembering where to go, it's about how you prepare and organise yourself: how you use your corners to set yourself up; how your short sides and half-halts are there to activate your horse and get it back in front of your leg; how important it is to ride your test accurately, marker to marker. But it was an attitude I was learning, too. Before, not being confident in what I was doing, I was always holding back. Now I felt I could experiment a bit more and take a risk, and that's when the marks started to go up.

Another thing I learned from Carl was how to travel: I'd had so little experience of flying and airports before. 'How do you know where to go? Where do I even look for the flight number?' 'Oh, Eddie, come on,' he'd say, and then off we'd go.

The experience I felt I was gaining and all the places I was getting to see made me feel incredibly lucky. It was all eye-opening, and thanks to Carl we always stayed in nice places and went to good restaurants. I'll never forget one fish restaurant in Saumur: it was in a beautiful location over the river in town, but at dinner

Carl ordered a hideous seafood platter with snails on it. Of course they're a really French thing to eat, but OMG it put me off my food.

Fritzens in Austria was another incredible experience: the competition is hosted by the Haim-Swarovski family and the trot-ups were held in the indoor school under the biggest chandeliers I'd ever seen in my entire life. We were even taken for a trip round the Swarovski crystal factory, although I was very good: I only looked.

Rocking up at Fritzens you literally feel like you're in heaven, the arena is so high up in the clouds. Then the sky clears and there are stunningly beautiful mountains all around. It's like you're in the middle of a stage-set for *Heidi*. We had another lovely hotel to go back to, also arranged by Carl, and while we were there we ended up being talked into trying the owner's home-brewed schnapps. For some reason, everyone but me seemed to think it was delicious stuff; I thought it tasted like poison. After three shots I felt like I was going to pass out, and as I knew I had to ride the next day, I managed to drag myself up to bed.

Fast-forward twelve hours and Blueberry and I went out and won the Grand Prix with nearly 78 per cent, so I decided to go and find the old hotelier again. My idea was to thank him, jokingly, for putting me in an alcoholic coma before I rode because I hadn't felt any nerves at all beforehand. I don't think the humour came across. The next thing I knew he was handing me a whole bottle of his hideous drink, which didn't please me or Carl, who was devastated he hadn't got one as well.

With Blueberry now qualified for the Europeans, I took Dez out to Aachen in July for the Nations' Cup. It was my first time riding on a team and I'd been selected partly to see how I dealt with the pressure. As

CHARLOTTE DUJARDIN

Carl had decided to give Uti a rest, I was alongside
Laura Bechtolsheimer, Emile Faurie and Richard
Davison, all riders who were much more experienced
than me. What I didn't know then was what a horrible
venue Aachen would turn out to be for me and Blueberry:
the atmosphere was intense, but that first time I was
just excited to be riding at yet another show I'd only
sat and watched at before.

Carl came out to Germany to warm me up, and I
finished eleventh in the Grand Prix and Special and
twelfth in the Freestyle. Laura was second in the Grand
Prix on Mistral Højris, but most of the attention was
on Totilas, who had been sold to Paul Schockemöhle
of Germany a few months earlier.

The storm Totilas's sale had caused had been unpre-
cedented. I felt sorry for Edward Gal to have lost the
horse he'd trained up from a young age and spent so
long developing a partnership with, and I also felt for
Matthias Rath, who had to pick up where Edward had
left off. The pressure he was under was horrendous: it
had taken Edward years and years to form the bond he
had with Totilas, and people seemed to expect Matthias
to reproduce the same thing overnight.

Buying and selling horses is just a fact of the sport.
I'd made up my mind about selling Dez if I ever got
him sound again, and when the Norwegian rider
Cathrine Rasmussen approached me after Aachen, I
knew Dez and I had got as far as we could together.
Part of being a good rider is taking into consideration
a horse's limits, and although Dez had gone far beyond
anyone's expectations, he just didn't have the same
ability as Blueberry had. I'd realised I was in danger
of pushing Dez the way I did Blueberry, and that
because he was so genuine he might injure himself
trying for me. I had to back off, and I knew Cathrine

120

would love Dez as much as I did. We agreed that she'd come to the yard before she took him away to learn his routine, and I was able to show her how much he loved having his back scratched and how he needed to be kissed and cuddled.

I knew it wasn't goodbye forever as I'd be seeing him again on the circuit, but on the day he went I was in bits. I said my goodbyes to him in the stable because I couldn't bear to see him be loaded on to the lorry, then I had to walk away and go to the cottage where I could sit on my own and cry my eyes out. One of the worst things was that Dez would always whinny for me when he saw me coming into the yard. Suddenly to have the place quiet and his stable empty was heart-breaking.

* * *

The dreams I'd had when I'd first started competing were now coming true, and at the 2011 Europeans I achieved the first of my goals. To have gone from stable girl to a member of the British team was one thing, but being on a team with Carl Hester was the icing on the cake.

As well as Carl, I would be riding alongside Laura Bechtolsheimer and Emile Faurie, and all of us had high expectations. I was being counted on to go out and deliver, which felt like a big ask, plus I had no idea how Blueberry would cope with the atmosphere. For me, the more people the better, but the stadium at Rotterdam was vast and the buzz incredible.

Mum came out to support me, and as Blueberry and I warmed up for the Grand Prix Carl was joking away in my earpiece, making me feel at ease. No matter how big the occasion he'll have me laughing before I go in, usually by saying things he really shouldn't. When it came to it, though, he could barely watch – the photographer Jon Stroud caught his reactions and half the time he was literally clinging to a pillar to keep upright. But Blueberry, like the genius he is, didn't bat an eyelid. We scored 78.83 per cent and when I came out Carl was actually crying with pride. It will stay with me forever, that moment: he gave me a massive hug and told me what a good job I'd done, which really took me aback. All I'd ever wanted was to make him proud of me, and knowing that I had was one of the most amazing feelings.

After that it was Carl's turn, and Uti was on fire: you thought he was going to break into a canter any second, his trot extensions were so huge. Everyone was holding on to their seats because Carl wasn't going to give a single mark away, and when he got to his final centre line and saluted it was just uproar. His 82.56 per cent was a personal best, and then when Laura and Mistral Højris came out with 77.28 per cent we knew we'd got the gold. Happy doesn't even begin to describe how I felt. To have won a team gold medal in my first year at Grand Prix and beaten the Germans and Dutch, all with a horse who was only nine, was just unbelievable. After we'd been given our medals we were taken to a stage in the arena where we were interviewed and presented with bottles of champagne, and it wasn't long before everyone was soaked.

Friday was a rest day, but the draw for the Special on the Saturday meant that Carl and I were riding too close together for him to help warm me up. Although he was keeping an eye on me as we were working in together, it wasn't quite the same, and I felt a little bit lost and insecure without him. We had a few blips, which were more down to the fact that Blueberry and I were still quite green than anything else, but managed to finish sixth, with Carl and Laura taking silver and bronze behind Adelinde Cornelissen on Parzival.

As ever, the top-ranked riders then went through to the Freestyle, but there I made a bit of a mess. For the first time the music I was riding to had been put together especially for me and it had only arrived the day before. I hadn't had time to practise, and I was so nervous that when the judges rang the bell, instead of putting my hand up to start the music, I saluted. Everybody was laughing at me and I ended up going wrong and having to make it up, so while Adelinde and Carl repeated their gold and silver, Blueberry and I ended up ninth.

* * *

To people seeing Blueberry and me for the first time in 2011, it probably did seem as though Carl was letting his working pupil ride his top horse. But what they didn't see was the way we worked together at home and how much of a team he and I had become. When I'd first started at Carl's, if he told me to jump, I'd ask how high. I'll never forget being given his phone number for the first time: I was grinning from ear to ear. But as Uti and Blueberry were starting to get more and more success we had started working on them together. I would ride first and Carl would sit down and help teach me, then I'd sit down and help him. It had become a pattern, and training both horses the way we did was obviously working.

As Carl had decided that I was the queen of trot (he's always been the king of canter), I'd taken over Uti's trot work at home and some of his piaffe/passage, partly to save Carl's back. Uti is a small horse but so bouncy. I loved riding him because he was a ball of fun, but his trot bashed you right up the rear end.

I liked to think that having me around was helping Carl to up his game a bit; I'm definitely not sure how much he had ever had anybody ordering him around before I came along. He loves to joke that our relationship is give and take – he gives advice and I have to take it – but I am who I am and when I'm training, I tell it how it is: it doesn't matter if you're Mark Todd, Carl Hester or anybody else. Black is black and white is white with me, and although Carl is an amazing rider and my absolute hero, if he starts curling his horse up to the left or swinging his body in his changes, I tell him. After years of being called 'Eddie' by him, I'd got my revenge and come up with my own nickname for him: 'Granddad'. Carl hated it, especially when I started using it in public, but if he wasn't going to stop, neither was I, and now we only ever call each other by our proper names if we're annoyed about something.

* * *

After I'd sold Fernandez I was in the fortunate position of being able to buy a house of my own. I wanted somewhere quite modern, with good views and close by to Carl's, but the few places I looked at locally needed quite a lot of work doing to them. I have to say, it's quite disheartening going to see houses, because they never look the same as they do on the internet – same as with horses, really.

Sandra Biddlecombe tipped me off about the house I live in now, which was then in the middle of being renovated. Its surroundings were so overgrown you couldn't even see it to begin with, just the wild forest that had grown up everywhere. But as soon as the renovations were finished and I walked into the kitchen for the first time, it instantly felt like home. The views are beautiful, Carl is five minutes down the road, and there's only an acre of land so I can lock up and go any time I want.

Buying your own house outright at twenty-six isn't something many people can do and I knew how very, very lucky I was. Added to that, being able to say I'd got my own home, after all that my mum and dad had gone through, was a huge relief. With their share of the money my parents were also able to pay off their mortgage, so after everything Fernandez had given me, he'd now given us all stability and financial security as well.

* * *

Having ridden at the Europeans, there was another thing I wanted to tick off my list for 2011: riding at Olympia. To me it's the best show in the world. You're in London, at Christmas time, in a place that's packed each night with 6,000 people who are pretty much close enough to reach out and touch you as you go round the outside. From a young girl, I'd been desperate to compete there. I'd go and watch the dressage each year and want to get into that arena so much I can't tell you. Sadly, the closest I'd got was one year when some showing friends had roped my parents into getting me and my sister involved in the parade finale. I wasn't even on a horse: I was dressed as a chicken and Emma-Jayne was a duck, and what either had got to do with Christmas I really don't know. My mum dyed some stockings a hideous luminous yellow, and every night for nearly a week we were down in that main arena, running around with Santa Claus.

My debut with Valegro was hopefully going to be a bit more dignified, so that meant getting new music for my Freestyle. The music for my test at the Europeans had been put together by a young composer called Tom Hunt, who had approached me after seeing Blueberry at Hickstead in July. Tom studied music at university and plays a lot of different instruments himself; when we talked I also liked the fact that he was open-minded and good at listening to what I wanted as a rider. The problem at the Europeans was that I'd ended up getting lost because there hadn't been enough of a distinction in the music between the different parts of my test. This time, I wanted to make sure there were little key musical indicators all the way through so I knew what I should be doing and where I should be. When you ride a Freestyle you really want the crowd to feel the music and be captivated by it. At Olympia not only did the people watching love my music, the judges really liked it too. Tom and I had decided to use the theme from the film *How to Train Your Dragon*, and as I was riding down the centre line all I could hear was click, click, click from the photographers. I could feel Blueberry almost physically growing into the occasion and the attention that was on him, and although I didn't make my halt at the beginning and we had a mistake in our twos, I had the time of my life. We finished second to Laura Bechtolsheimer – she got 83.975 per cent and I got 83.7 per cent, which was my second personal best in two days: the night before I'd won the Grand Prix and broken the 80 per cent barrier for the first time, scoring 81.043 per cent. It had been my first time out with Blueberry since the Europeans, and it was almost as if he was saying to me, 'Let's do this,' because for the first time I remember we went into that Grand Prix and came back with a clear round.

Seeing Dez in action with Cathrine added to the magic, and Carl and Laura were also having an amazing show. Laura's win with Mistral Højris (Alf) in the Freestyle made her the first British rider ever to win the Olympia World Cup Qualifier, and Carl and Uti also hit 83 per cent. It was a great way for all of us to end the year, one that for me had been nothing less than mind-blowing. It was only nine months since I'd been scoring 73 per cent at my first international Grand Prix and now here we were hitting the 80s. And, with the London Olympics only eight months in the future, the buzz about our medal chances had really begun.

* * *

Christmas 2011 was the first one I'd ever spent away from my family. It had always been such a big occasion for us that it felt weird not being at home, but at the same time I almost felt like I had a second family with Dean and Carl and everyone at the yard. One vital new member of our team was Alan Davies, who had begun as our travelling groom in March and who, as far as I'm concerned, is the best groom in the whole world. He's got years of experience and knows everything, so if I ever get stuck I ring him up and he tells me exactly what to do. Not only that, he's the most incredible supporter and so proud of what our horses achieve. I've often seen him biting his lip after tests, trying not to cry, because he knows we'll take the mick out of him if he does. He's definitely the key to my success because he never stresses, and even if things do go wrong he just deals with it calmly so Carl and I can get on with our jobs. Knowing my horses are in the best hands gives me huge confidence, and when Blueberry began 2012 by flying out to Wellington in Florida for the World Dressage Masters, it put my mind at ease to know Alan would be with him. I had no idea how Blueberry would take to flying, but it didn't surprise me when Alan told me afterwards he just ate the whole way.

Before Carl and I flew out ourselves we had to do a photoshoot for the competition programme at Carl's house. I had my hair and make-up done, then I had to get dressed up in lots of weird clothes that I'd never have chosen to wear: frilly shirts and skirts and things that weren't me at all. The girls who were there to help us were lovely, but I was so out of my comfort zone, I just wanted to dig a hole and get in it. By the time I found myself having to pretend to kiss a frog ornament I was just about dying inside, especially playing the sidekick to Carl, who was obviously the supermodel of the pair of us.

I hadn't been to America before and one of the first things I noticed about it was the food: the portion sizes were insane. I ordered a salad for dinner one night and had to ask if it was really all for me; calorie-wise, I might as well have ordered a burger and chips, the amount of sauce it had on it. The facilities were like nothing I'd ever seen before, either: the luxury out there is unbelievable. The stable yards look like people's houses, and the houses go for millions and millions. Then we went for a trip to Palm Beach and all you could see were Ferraris.

Having had a few days' rest to recover from the flight, Blueberry was raring to go. The atmosphere for the Grand Prix was electric and he was so excited I could barely hold him. By the time we'd completed the first movements he was already pulling my arms out, and I almost had to stand up in my stirrups for the half-passes, he was so strong.

It definitely felt like he had taken charge, and although we finished second with 78 per cent, I was pretty disappointed because I knew we could do much better. For the Freestyle I wanted to make sure I was the one in control, but for some reason we had started struggling with clapping. Blueberry had done quite a few prize-givings by now and the noise of applause when we entered the arena would get him so excited he wouldn't always remember he was meant to be doing a test.

Given how fresh he was, I was worried going into the Freestyle about whether I'd actually be able to halt him to do my salute. It ended up being blink-and-you'll miss it – stop, raise your hand, go: no hanging around – but we made it, and although our 83 per cent put us second again, I was much happier this time as I knew I'd done a better job.

In both the Freestyle and the Grand Prix, first place went to the American rider Steffen Peters with his horse Ravel. The marks the two of us were awarded caused some controversy, and Steffen had even come over to congratulate me after the Freestyle, thinking I'd won. However, the American judge ended up giving Blueberry and me less than 80 per cent, while Steffen got a much higher mark. I hadn't seen his test so I didn't really know if that was fair or not, but as it came down to something I had no control over, I wasn't going to worry about it. What mattered to me was that I'd done my best and enjoyed myself.

Carl had left Uti at home and was riding Fiona Bigwood's horse Wie Atlantico. Fiona was pregnant so had offered Carl the ride, and they were both delighted when he came fourth in the Freestyle riding to his favourite Tom Jones medley. That music was Granddad to a tee: he'd been using it for years and it was cheesy as sin. We were all trying to hint gently that he might want to have a change, but I decided it was up to me to insist, and thank goodness he got Tom Hunt to compose his music for London 2012.

One of the most dramatic images from Wellington was of Blueberry rearing up in the prize-giving: a horse had bashed into him seconds before and he went up in the air. It's a picture I hate because he'd never, ever reared or bucked in his life before: he'd only done it because he was genuinely frightened and it wasn't a fair impression at all of his character or the horse that he was.

As soon as Carl and I were back from Florida, the Olympics began to seem a lot more real. I wouldn't know until much nearer the time if I'd been selected, but it seemed sensible to prepare in view of the year I'd had. Carl's plan was for both of us to concentrate on training at home with a run-out at Hagen in May. Horse & Country filmed our preparations in the series *Carl and Charlotte: Dressage Superstars*. Viewers were duly treated to the delights of one of our training sessions, which was absolutely typical in that Carl made me ride down the centre line about a hundred times. It's the way we always work together: I do something and he'll tell me to pat the horse, slap myself and do it again. Even if I think I've done something well, he'll find something wrong, because what it looks like and what it feels like can be completely different. We'll have little rows about it sometimes, which is why when we do demonstrations he never lets me have a mic – he doesn't like me being able to answer him back. We end up doing things again, and again, and again, but that's what dressage is all about: discipline and perfection. Whenever I practise bits of my test Carl will sit at the top of the arena calling out marks, and every time he calls out 'Seven' I'm so cross at myself. 'Seven? Seven?! I don't want a seven! I want a nine or a ten!'

But for all the preparation there are things that you are never going to be able to plan for, and a few days before Hagen, Uti managed to pull his shoe off in the field. Unfortunately Uti has always been a horse with sensitive feet, and so although he only needed a few days off, Carl had to withdraw.

He was gutted, as was I, because this was going to have been a chance for us both to go against the Germans – the riders who, along with the Dutch, would be our main rivals for gold in Greenwich. But there was nothing to be done, so although Carl came along for support, it was just me and Blueberry who would be riding out into the lion's den.

Much of the attention was on Matthias and Totilas, who were looking stronger than they had done in Rotterdam now they'd had time to develop as a combination. It made you feel quite sorry for Matthias because he couldn't ride anywhere without people taking pictures and filming him and criticising him on social media, but although it must have been quite difficult to deal with, he handled it really well. Kristina Sprehe and Desperados were another combination really starting to come through for the Germans, but as well as getting a sense of what we were up against in terms of the opposition, one of the main aims of riding at Hagen was to practise the new test for the Special. It had been shortened for the London Olympics to take account of TV coverage and the number of riders, and, as it would also now count towards the team results, it was vital to have a run-through.

Until the Europeans, I hadn't really felt as though I knew what I was doing a lot of the time. I'd get one bit of my test good, then straight away I'd lose another bit. Now, things finally felt like they were coming together and my test was a lot more secure, so although I was in Germany – the danger zone – I didn't really feel any pressure.

In the build-up to big competitions my preparation never varies. It begins the night or morning before when I'll watch a DVD of an old test or training session with Carl on my iPad so I can see where I'm weak and also get the feel in my body of what I need to be doing.

Sometimes it's only by seeing myself that I can completely understand what Carl has been telling me, plus hearing him screaming at me means that when I am on my own, what I need to do comes almost automatically because I can still hear his voice in my head.

Then the final hour or so before warming up I'll spend with Ian in the lorry. Ian has got a playlist on his phone that we've put together over the years and we'll have a little boogie together: the tunes are all sorts, but one of my favourites is 'Everybody's Free (To Wear Sunscreen)' by Baz Luhrmann. I'd been at school when it came out and my best friend Kayleigh had been so obsessed with it she'd copied out all the lyrics, but it's a philosophy I like too. don't worry about the future, because worrying won't get you anywhere. I've never seen the point in over-thinking things before competitions – it's better to go in relaxed, with a clear mind. Then Ian pins my stock on, makes sure my hair isn't a mess, and we're off.

In Hagen, Blueberry won the Grand Prix with 81 per cent, which felt like a good result given the combinations we were up against, but then the warm-up for the Special turned into an absolute disaster.

The warm-up arena was next to the shade of some trees, and because it was a hot day there were flies everywhere. I'd told Alan that Blueberry would need lots of fly spray, but flies were still touching his nose and his head shaking came back with a vengeance. He was starting to get into a white lather because he was so stressed out, and even the other horses and riders coming at us were scaring him and making him try to run away.

I knew I had to walk him, to try and get him to calm down, but as if that wasn't bad enough the batteries in the headset Carl was using to talk to me went flat, so then he started stressing out too. We managed to borrow a headset, but when I started to canter, Carl suddenly told me I was doing my changes on the wrong rein. Because it was a new test I panicked, and by the time Carl realised he was wrong and I was right, I had the heebie-jeebies badly because I didn't think I was going to be able to remember anything at all. So much for being relaxed with a clear mind.

Ian had come to support me, and I looked at him and said, 'I'm going to go wrong.' But Ian being Ian he reassured me, told me to take a breath, then got me to speak the test back to him even though at this point we only had moments left.

It was all so stressful outside that when I got into that arena it was actually a relief: peace and quiet. There was no one screaming at me or stressing, I could just go and ride, and I didn't make a single mistake the whole way round. Blueberry's ones had always been the patchiest part of my test because they were so big, and in warm-ups I often couldn't get them. But whenever we got into the arena it was as though he knew how important this was. I don't even know how I did it: fifteen ones on the diagonal. As I hit the board, I literally did my last change, and all I could think was, 'Wow.' Carl had been yelling at me for so long that I didn't move my legs fast enough and I had to be quicker, but holy moly did I ride those one-time changes in Hagen!

Thinking back now it still gives me goosebumps, because when I finished everyone was on their feet, giving me a standing ovation. I looked at the scoreboards, tens were coming up, then people were running from everywhere to congratulate me. I'd scored 88.022 per cent: a new world record, beating the previous record of 86.46 per cent set by Totilas and Edward Gal in 2010. Matthias had decided to compete Totilas in the Freestyle instead of the Special, but we were still over 9 per cent ahead of the second-placed rider, Anna Kasprzak.

Anabel Balkenhol finished third and Isabell Werth was fourth, and afterwards we were all taken off to do press and media. Sitting next to Isabell is one of the things I remember best about that press conference, and other thing is being asked by one of the reporters how I coped with my nerves.

'Well,' I said, 'it's the same old stuff and just another arena.' Whenever I'm competing I visualise myself going down the centre line as though I'm at home; just because I'm not doesn't make any difference to what I'm doing. In fact, riding in the arena at a competition is always less scary for me than riding at home, because at home it's Carl sitting in the judge's box.

Everyone laughed as I tried to explain, but afterwards Anabel came up to me. Her dad is Klaus Balkenhol, who is an extremely talented trainer and rider himself, but I know Anabel had had problems with her nerves. 'How you deal with it – it's so true,' she said. I think maybe I'd opened her eyes to a way of thinking she'd never encountered before, but I knew from experience that if I got nervous, that's when things started to go wrong.

I'm not sure I can say how it feels to break a world record, because the truth is I was in a bit of a daze. Granddad and I were both taken aback when we saw the score I'd got, and although I had everybody round me, hugging me and telling me 'well done' – Carl, Ian, Dr Bechtolsheimer – I didn't actually believe it.

It was only when I got back to the lorry with Ian that what I'd achieved really sank in: 'OH MY GOD! I'VE JUST GOT A WORLD RECORD!' We were both absolutely ecstatic – and, of all places, it had happened in Germany. How was that even possible? Wow. Just ... wow.

9

The Girl on the Dancing Horse

EACH YEAR THE 'Horses and Dreams' show at Hagen has a theme, and in 2012 the theme was Britain, in honour of the London Olympics. During one of the prize-givings, the music from *The Great Escape* was playing in the background. 'That would be really good music to use for your London Freestyle,' Ian said to me – and that's how it all began.

I'm probably more picky than some riders about their music, but I don't want to ride to anything that I don't like or that I feel doesn't do my horse justice. Everybody's got their own personal preference, but good music is fitted to the type of horse you've got, and because Blueberry was so powerful, I knew I wanted something dramatic as well as something that told a story.

Tom Hunt had come and recorded me riding so he could work on Blueberry's previous music: having seen his footfalls, he could then work on finding rhythms that matched. Having music that exactly fits a horse's particular movements is what makes for the best Freestyles, and that's Tom's specialty. Even so he'd go away and do something, send it back to me, and some bits of it I'd like and some bits I'd hate. He must have wanted to pull his hair out the first few times we worked together, because he'd get halfway through and I'd tell him to start again.

It was the same with my music for London. 'I need more definition in the piaffe, Tom, and I really want to hear the difference between my extended trot and my normal trot. Oh, and can I get the Big Ben bells for the pirouettes?'

Off he'd go and work on it some more, and it would come back with some bits that I loved and some bits that still weren't right. Carl and I had decided that the international at Hartpury on 6 July would be my test-run for London, but with a week to go, Tom was still making tweaks. Two days to go – nothing. One day to go – no CD. He finally drove down with it on the day of my test, so the first time I heard my Olympic music in full was as I rode in to compete in front of a sell-out house.

People often think I've practised to perfection before I go in to ride my Freestyle, but I honestly haven't. The Grand Prix and Special are what count in terms of qualifying and team results, so those are the ones you work on. It might sound odd, but thinking about music for a Freestyle is something that a lot of us tend to leave to last.

The Olympics opening ceremony was now exactly three weeks away and, wouldn't you know, the weather for Hartpury was torrential rain. I got soaked right the way through and the arena was so wet and disgusting that I thought if Blueberry and I could get round on a day like that, we could get round anything – you never know with English weather, but whatever happened in London, at least I was prepared.

We won the Grand Prix with 81.66 per cent, and then it was on to the Freestyle which, luckily, was indoors as part of a gala evening. I was a bit on edge because I'd received my music so late and just wanted to focus, but Blueberry felt great.

Carl had decided not to compete Uti so that he could concentrate on helping me – he knew at the Olympics

I'd be the one everyone was relying on to bring in the big score. Having ridden at other Olympics he also knew what was to come and the kind of pressure I'd be under, but as I went into that final run-through I was more excited than nervous. My mum had come to watch, and Hartpury, which is just down the road from the yard, is an arena I always love riding in. Then my music started and it was as if I'd been riding to it forever. If I'd told anybody I'd had it for less than a day, they'd never have believed me. When Blueberry and I came out it was with 90.65 per cent – my first time riding to my new music, my first 90 per cent score and a British record.

When I look back now, one of the things I regret about my career is never really celebrating much. It sounds silly but by the time you've ridden, done all the press and the media, returned to the lorry, changed and got back to your hotel, you're exhausted: all you want is to have dinner and go to bed. You're either at a show, travelling home from a show, or getting ready for another show: that's your life. Even after my world record in Hagen, I'd been so overwhelmed by what I had coming up that I didn't have time to dwell on what I'd just accomplished.

At Hartpury I wasn't taking it in my stride – afterwards I celebrated properly. Tom came back to my house together with Ian and my sister, while Dean ended up doing handstands and cartwheels and all sorts in the garden. It went on so late and got so messy that eventually I told the boys I was leaving them to it and went to bed exhausted. It was not a pretty sight in the morning, I can tell you.

The official phone call from Dickie Waygood, our Chef d'Equipe, came not long after that: I had made the team along with Carl and Laura, and Richard

Davison would be riding as an individual. It wasn't a surprise because I knew I was one of the strongest team contenders, but to have it confirmed ... '*Damn!*' I thought. 'I've made it!' You know when you've imagined something as a kid, and dreamed of it for so long, and then it actually happens? I was going to the Olympics! I kept walking around saying it to myself: 'Oh my God, I'm going to the Olympics. Oh. My. God.'

Even so, I didn't want to get too excited because I knew something might still happen, as it was happening for Carl. Every time Uti was shod he got sore feet, which meant Carl had to back off his training for a couple of days. Carl is used to reassuring me when I start panicking and think I can't do something – 'Oh, Eddie, you always say that and you always pull it off' – but this time the tables were turned. I tried to be upbeat, but we were both relying on Haydn Price, our amazing team farrier. Haydn retired after Rio in 2016 and is hugely missed by us all. Not only was he fantastic at his job, he was also down there by the ring at every competition, cheering us on, and lighting the place up with his amazing smile.

Haydn was part of what Carl called 'the British army': the team of experts the World Class Performance Programme had put in place to help us go for gold. Mark Fisher, our saddle fitter, came to watch me and Blueberry and used a special saddle pad and vest fitted with motion sensors so that we could see what I was doing with my body and how I distributed my weight. He was even making tiny adjustments to our saddles while we were in London, to make sure they were perfectly balanced. The information he'd gleaned, he passed on to Andy Thomas, our physio. Like Jo Theyer, the difference Andy made to my riding was incredible. One of my biggest problems was that my right glute didn't really fire whereas my left was really tight, and when Andy started working on me, the words that came out of my mouth I can't actually write here. Many's the time we were the comedy double act at competitions: Andy would set up his temporary physio room and by the time he'd finished leaning his whole body weight on my butt cheek, I'd be swearing and screaming so much people would stop outside the curtain and wonder what on earth was going on.

Blueberry also has a physio, Marnie Campbell, although his massages are nice, relaxing ones he gets to sleep through. Marnie isn't part of World Class but she's essential to our team and has the incredible skill of being able to pick up with her hands what I've felt as I've been riding without me needing to say a word. With all these people along with our team vet John McEwen, it felt like we were leaving nothing to chance. There was no room for error and we were all working together in the build-up to Greenwich, which is what it's all about when the pressure is on.

The next step on the road to London was a team visit to the NEC in Birmingham to receive our kit. Getting my Team GB clothing was one of the best days of my life: we each had a personal dresser to help us and by the end I had so many bags I had to wheel them out to my car on a trolley. Ian, who was going to be helping me in London, also got a kit (Carl calls him my 'lady in waiting'), although not all the clothes were things you'd necessarily have chosen to wear. Being in trainers for vets' inspections and trot-ups wasn't ideal because there was always the worry that your horse would get excited and jump on your foot and break your toes, and as for the men's white and gold tracksuits ... all I can say is: Ali G. I'm used to seeing Carl and Richard in quite smart clothes, but when the two of them came out of the changing rooms it was like the gangstas had rolled into town.

With Blueberry, Uti and Alf we knew we had three horses who could hit 80 per cent. That meant if we all got our best scores, we could get gold – and, as favourites, that was what was expected of us. However, the competition was going to be fierce: the Germans were without Matthias and Totilas, and Isabell had decided not to compete as Don Johnson wasn't at full fitness. But one of the reasons why the Germans have always been top of the game is that they don't just have one or two stars, they've got real strength in depth. Kristina Sprehe on Desperados would definitely be one to beat, but Helen Langehanenberg on Damon Hill was in great form. He was a liver chestnut stallion, beautiful to look at, and on their day the two of them could pull off a really good test and show many highlights. Then for the Dutch there was Adelinde and Parzival, and Edward Gal on his new horse Undercover. Anky van Grunsven had also come out of retirement to compete in her seventh Olympics. Although I tried not to think about it in that way, there wasn't a combination that wasn't a threat, because after all these were the best riders in the world.

By the time we arrived in Greenwich, the Olympics had already begun and the British medals were starting to come in. We were staying in the Novotel in Greenwich instead of the Olympic Village, and because World Class had booked the whole of it out for us it was like our own little British camp. One of the tough things about being at an Olympics is being separated from your friends and family, but in the Novotel we could have them with us. A short walk away was the team house, where we could have physio or just chill out and watch

TV, and we only had to go five minutes down the road to be at the venue.

The warmth of the atmosphere was amazing. Everyone was so friendly and enthusiastic and there were lots of familiar faces: people I knew from British Dressage; Jennie Loriston-Clarke, who was volunteering as a steward, and Judy Harvey, who was commentating for the BBC. As for the surroundings, you couldn't have wished for more. Greenwich Park is a gorgeous space, and everything had been done to reduce the environmental impact, even down to raising up the stables so that the horses' urine didn't damage the grass. The main arena, which was in the Old Royal Naval College, was just stunning, although riding with Canary Wharf in the background felt a bit surreal compared to the usual indoor school.

The Olympic equestrian events had kicked off with the eventers, who were winning their team silver as we arrived in London. Our timetable also overlapped with the showjumpers' and I found it fascinating to watch how other riders coped and dealt with the pressure. The other disciplines are a different kettle of fish from us: dressage can be a bit uptight, but jumpers as a whole are much cooler. They like a drink and a party and don't worry what colour bandages their horse is wearing or if all their clothes match. The eventers are just hardcore, as you would be with three different disciplines to deal with. In any sport you've got to take risks, but with cross-country riding you've got to be really brave and gutsy. A lot of the time I'd be watching them and thinking, 'Oh my God, are you really going to jump *that*?'

Carl was now feeling the pressure as Team GB went from strength to strength: not only was he the most senior rider, he was also our coach. One evening we all went for a meal at a pub in Greenwich, just a stroll from the Novotel. I ordered a big, fat, juicy steak because I thought I needed all the protein and energy I could get in view of what was to come, and as were eating we discussed winning gold. By the end of the evening we'd agreed we'd just do the best we could, but I'm sure Carl kept a lot of what he was really thinking to himself. He didn't want me to feel nervous or worried, but each morning I'd come out from my room to find he hadn't slept a wink. In fact, most of the time he looked absolutely terrified. I really think he probably would have gone home if he could, whereas I was bouncing off the walls like a big kid.

Even now, what I'd achieved to be there in London seems crazy. There had been people along the way who told me I'd never be successful simply because I didn't have enough money, and I'd thought: 'I don't care, you're not going to stop me, I'm just going to keep trying.' And now I'd done it. I was on an Olympic team through dedication and sheer hard work.

That was why I wanted to make sure I came away from London with no regrets. I didn't want to leave an Olympics thinking about things I wished I'd done, so I set out to make sure I ticked every box: to go out and enjoy every minute, to mix with other nations and athletes, to take in every last bit of the atmosphere.

One of the things I loved was swapping pins with other nations' athletes. Every country has a different pin, and the idea is to trade as many as you can and wear them on your lanyard. Some of the older riders weren't bothered and didn't really take part, but I found it so much fun and a great way of meeting and talking to new people.

By now, having seen everyone else ride and lived it all with them, I was really excited. It's not often we get the chance to ride in front of so many people and I just wanted to get going, but Carl had decided with the selectors that I was going to be riding last, on the second day of the Grand Prix. Normally it's the most experienced riders who go last, but Carl had wanted to ride first so he was free to help me prepare. That meant Laura had to ride second, which I think she was a bit unhappy about, as she and Alf were more experienced than me. But Carl knew Blueberry was reliable and that if I did well I could get the biggest score.

That I took the news so calmly shocked him a little. As the last to go, I'd have to make things up if anybody had a bad round, and if we'd done well, it would be my job to make sure we got the gold. But even though this was the Olympics, my philosophy didn't change: I looked at it as though it was a normal show, and my start time was just my start time.

We each had our own little different routines and ways of managing. Laura had her family around to support her, and I stuck to my schedule of physio with Andy in the mornings and then a walk over to the stables to stretch Blueberry. My plan was to do nothing differently, but when it came down to actually watching Carl ride, all my calm went out of the window. I'd helped him warm up and for some reason Uti had started to take over from Carl so that every time he went into extended canter, Uti put in a flying change. Carl is a genius in the arena but he can get quite worried outside it so I didn't want to say too much and make the situation worse, but my heart was pounding through my chest watching him and I think I rode every single stride of that test with him in my head.

Unfortunately Uti did the same thing again in the arena, but otherwise theirs was a great test for 77.72 per cent. Laura had a few mistakes and was a bit disappointed with her 76.83 per cent, and although she and Carl finished day one first and second, I knew that without an 80 per cent there was work for me to do.

One of the things that had worried Laura was the sheer volume of the applause from the 20,000-strong crowd: for a lot of the horses it was proving to be quite scary, especially because you had to enter the arena through a narrow chute between two of the mountainous stands. I was worried as well, but these were people who had come to support us and of course they wanted to show their feelings. If Blueberry reacted, I thought, I'd just have to deal with it and do my best to reassure him.

I'd had a chance to look at the arena once before, at a rehearsal event in 2011 designed to test how the surface stood up. But when I rode in for real, it felt completely different: the stands were ginormous, but you were so far away from everyone and it was so silent that it was almost like you were out there riding on your own.

My plan was to enter at walk to let Blueberry see what he could see, and as he did suddenly take it all in, I could feel he was slightly surprised. He definitely tensed up under me, but I just patted him on the neck and as I did I literally felt him take a breath and relax. It was an amazing feeling – that he trusted me so much and had such confidence in me – and I don't know why, but I was immediately reassured. I went in determined to nail my test, although I almost fell at the first hurdle. It wasn't until I came out that I discovered I was one second away from a time fault: I'd only just made it into the arena within the permitted forty-five seconds. Afterwards, I pretended I'd been playing it cool, but I think I had everybody absolutely losing their hair.

We moved off from halt and as we did what I felt most of all was that Blueberry was ready for this performance. We both were. I couldn't hear anything, couldn't see anything around me, all I was thinking about was what I was doing and the things Carl had told me in the months and years leading up to this moment.

One of the early dangers was the transition from passage to canter, because sometimes Blueberry would just shoot off when I put my leg on. This time there wasn't a hitch. After that, it was straight into my twos: I could always get them pretty well, but because they were worth double marks, and because I knew Blueberry was capable of getting a nine or ten in them, every one had to be bang on. I always gave Blueberry a little pat after we'd got our twos, and I wasn't going to change that even if we were at the Olympic Games. The canter extension was just a feeling of the most incredible power, but after that it was my canter zigzag. When you're watching it looks easy, but it's one of the hardest moves to ride. There's so much to think about – counting the strides, getting your changes, making sure you've got the same bend in each direction, keeping the quality of the canter – and again, it's a times two, so any error is costly. This time I finished a bit too close to the boards so Blueberry had to back off slightly at the very end and my last change was short. That meant my ones had to be perfect – and they were. But with those under my belt, and my right pirouette out of the way, I could feel myself starting to smile. I went for my final trot extension, pushed, and Blueberry just went: 'Yes! Let's go!' I could hear Granddad in my head, yelling, 'Hold it! Not too much, Eddie! Slow down!' but we were nearly there. Just that final centre line, which I've always loved: putting together that lovely passage, piaffe, passage transition, and the feeling you get of coming home. We had a tiny blip at the beginning, but then we halted and that was it. 'Holy moly!' I thought. 'I've just done the Olympics!'

We'd got 83.663 per cent, including twelve tens. That meant Team GB were in gold medal position, but the Dutch and the Germans were right behind: Adelinde had notched up 81.68 per cent, and Helen Langehanenberg had got 81.14 per cent. I knew both of them were massively strong contenders, but I tried not to get wrapped up in the hype. The way I work has always been to keep in my own little zone with the people closest to me – Carl, Ian and Alan – and anything or anybody that's going to make me feel negative, I try to keep away from.

The Grand Prix done and dusted, there were now three days to wait until the Special on Tuesday when the team medals would be decided. We all watched the British showjumpers win gold, their first medal for sixty years, but for our horses the long weekend was time off. Once you're at any big competition all your main preparation has been done and it's only panic that makes you feel like you should be changing things or keep on practising parts of your test. Realising that and being able to cope with it mentally is what is important, so I wasn't going to over-think things, although when Tuesday actually dawned, I was starting to feeling the pressure.

The Special was a test I'd practised much less than the Grand Prix, plus I had to do two sets of one-changes. Again I was last to go, and with Laura getting 77.79 per cent, and Carl hitting 80.57 per cent, I rode in knowing I had to deliver, I had to finish the job. We were so close to that gold – less than seven minutes away – but it would all depend on what I did next.

The Special was always quite a good test for Blueberry because it had lots of extended trots, for which he often scored tens. I wasn't going out there to break records, though: I wanted a safe clear round. That's how it felt most of the way – safe and solid – but as we went from the collected walk to the piaffe, Blueberry was keen and slightly anticipated the transition. We had a tiny hesitation going into the last piaffe, but the biggest blip was in the first set of one-time changes, where we had a short one. As I halted, I really didn't know if I'd done enough: it hadn't felt as polished as the Grand Prix, and I didn't know what those little errors were going to cost us. But I smiled and waved to that vast crowd, and I think it must have been then that I managed to catch a glimpse of the scoreboard: 83.29 per cent. I put my hand on my heart and looked up to the sky, thanking God and thanking Blueberry, because I knew that was it. I'd won Britain's twentieth gold medal of the London Olympics and our first-ever medal in dressage.

Receiving those medals was insane: it was the coolest moment ever. To ride into that arena, with that sea of British flags and that roar of clapping and cheering – it was so exciting. And such a proud moment: Britain had actually done it and it was the Germans and the Dutch who were behind us and following us in, which was pretty much unheard of. All three of us, Carl, Laura and I, were lapping it up, and our horses were going wild. Alf was so excited he was practically having to be held down. I made sure Fiona Lawrence, our yard manager, kept me far enough away from the others because Uti was spinning round and I was quite worried Blueberry might be kicked when we stopped. We dismounted and there was a human hedge of cameramen and photographers lined up waiting for us – the clicking was like nothing I'd ever heard. All of them were yelling: 'Charlotte! Look this way!' 'Charlotte, over here!' – you didn't know what you were meant to be doing. I looked at Laura and we had a little laugh because both of us were hoicking our breeches down: it's not good to have a photo that's going to appear round the world if you've got a camel toe, is it?

Our names were called and we climbed up onto the podium and I went cold and shivery and goosebumpy, hearing that crowd cheer for us. So many people were there for me that day – Dean, my mum, my dad, my sister, my brother who never came to shows (and his wife), the Dockleys, some of my friends from school – and it was that, for me, which made it so special. So much of my journey my parents hadn't physically been able to be a part of and had just watched on the computer, but knowing they were there to watch me get my medal made it feel like my story was complete. And to have Carl standing next to me: before the National Anthem I turned to hug him, the person who'd given up so much for me, and believed in me enough to make my dreams come true.

I couldn't believe how heavy that medal was as it was hung round my neck, but I picked it up and gave it a jolly good kiss to prove to myself it was real and I'd done it. Then 'God Save the Queen' began and I broke into the biggest grin because it felt like every single person in that stadium was singing.

I was so, so proud of Blueberry and of myself, to have achieved what we'd just achieved at our very first Olympics and won gold for our country. But of course it wasn't over yet: there was still the Freestyle to come.

We didn't want to do too much with any of the horses the following day, so we gave them a little stretch and took them up to the canter track that had been built for the eventers through Greenwich Park. Then Blueberry and I had a little schooling session with Carl, to run through a few of the lines. It was while we were walking back to the hotel that we were stopped by some mounted policemen who wanted to have a photograph taken with us. It was the funniest thing. There they were, just minding their business and getting on with their job, and suddenly they were stopping us and wanting photos. That was the amazing thing about competing at an Olympics in your home country: it felt like literally everyone you met, from people on the street to the army security guys, were with you.

Back in my room, I watched my test from Hartpury over and over: Tom and I had made a few tweaks to the music since then, so there were going to be a few bits of it I'd never ridden to before. Maybe that might have worried some people, but I loved that music so much, it fitted the surroundings so well, and I knew it was going to be such a crowd-pleaser, that I just couldn't wait for everyone to hear it and to see me and Blueberry in action.

Thursday arrived and it was obvious from the clear blue skies that it was going to be hot – really hot. Blueberry isn't great in the heat, which was a worry for me, but I also felt sorry for Carl because I knew he'd have to sweat a bit more than usual. Uti hasn't got the most stamina and by now he was definitely running out of fuel.

Of the eighteen riders who had gone forward to the Freestyle, I would be riding last, straight after Adelinde. Laura had been drawn fifteenth and Carl sixteenth, which meant there wasn't going to be a chance for me to help him prepare.

Laura pulled off a great score of 84.339 per cent riding to her Lion King music, and it was clear as I began my warm up that she was going to be a medal contender, but I had no idea what was happening in the main arena as Carl began his test – I could just hear the storm of noise as he rode in. As soon as he'd finished, he bypassed the media and came running over. I'll always remember the sight of him because he was bright red and sweat was literally running down his face, he was so hot. 'How did it go?' I asked, and I can't actually repeat what he said because it wasn't very polite. Uti had made him work hard for it, but he'd got 82.857 per cent, which would be enough for fifth.

Now it was my turn. I was pleased with the way Blueberry felt, and we'd practised our ones, which was the thing I'd been most worried about. When I'd been designing the test Carl had told me to do the minimum, eleven, because he knew I shouldn't push my luck. I didn't feel under any pressure now that I was just riding for myself and not the team, but as I was going in Adelinde's score flashed up on the giant scoreboard: 88.196 per cent. That made it a bit harder, knowing I had such a big score to beat, but as I was riding round the outside I kept reminding myself that all I could do was my best.

I entered, halted, then moved off straight into *The Great Escape* theme and my passage and piaffe. I hadn't got quite far enough up the arena to be exactly on my music as I turned for the extended trot to the James Bond theme from *Live and Let Die*, but it was only out by a fraction. Then it was the passage half-pass one way, into a trot half-pass the other way, where I always had to be careful not to canter because the aid is so similar with my outside leg going back behind the girth. I was concentrating so hard, but even as I was out there, in the middle of it all, my music made me feel so at home, so relaxed, so in the moment, that I was enjoying myself too – I felt totally in the zone with Blueberry.

As I was approaching the halfway point, Judy Harvey, who was in the commentary box with Mike Tucker, was I think feeling the heat. 'If ever there's a time to ride for your life, it's now, Charlotte,' she said to the viewers at home. Well, I was, Judy. In the collected walk to 'I Vow to Thee, My Country', encouraging Blueberry to get the relaxation was another challenge, but with that and my trot work out of the way, I now had to nail the canter. We had a tiny mistake in the zigzag where Blueberry made the change before me, but I wasn't too worried about it because it barely showed and we got it right the next time. My goal had always been to give Blueberry a nice ride and try and keep him confident, but as we were going from 'Land of Hope and Glory' and the extended canter into the final pirouettes to the chimes of Big Ben, I could feel him beginning to tire. He was still only ten, it was a sweltering afternoon, and he'd never had to work as hard as he'd had to over the past ten days. My one-times went without a hitch and at that point I was starting to feel really happy, but with Blueberry now flagging, I began to click to encourage him. And that was when it happened. As we went into the final piaffe ahead of the pirouette I clicked at him with my tongue to make the transition but he didn't quite get it. I brought him back and clicked again and he cantered again.

I completely and utterly blame myself because Blueberry is so sensitive that it was my clicking that had made him panic and shoot forward. Then I'd done it again and he'd got nervous again, so it absolutely wasn't his fault. We finished the final pirouette, halted, and at that point my emotions were mixed: I felt a little bit annoyed with myself because I'd made a mess of the end, but happy because I thought the rest of the test had gone well. I decided I'd done the best I could, and Blueberry physically could not have done any more, but then I rode out and I saw Carl's expression. He looked so disappointed. As he came over he said, 'That just cost you the gold.'

I can honestly say when I rode into that arena I'd never even thought of winning gold. With Adelinde having such a massive score I'd thought getting any medal at all would be amazing, but the feeling that I'd let Carl down was just gutting. I was deflated.

The minute I rode out Blueberry had to have his tack and bit checked. All the horses have to be checked over to make sure you haven't used any prohibited equipment. Carl, Ian, Dickie and Alan were all there with me in the 'kiss and cry' area at the back of the grandstands, and I don't think any of them could bear it as we waited for my score. Then the next thing I knew, a woman appeared over the top of one of the stands and was leaning down towards us. She was peering down because she was so high up, but what she was yelling was, 'YOU'VE DONE IT! YOU'VE DONE IT!' I'd got 90.089 per cent. And then the whole place erupted.

The noise was so loud, and so sudden, it caught me and Blueberry both by surprise and he shot forward. Then I burst into tears and fell down onto his neck: he didn't know what we'd just done, and I couldn't tell him in words, but I could hug him and try and show him how grateful I was.

People had asked me in the run-up to London if I'd cry if I got gold and I'd always said, no, why would I? I'd be happy. But in the past few minutes I'd gone from never imagining it was possible to thinking I'd completely blown it, and now I was an absolute emotional wreck. I still can't watch that test back because it makes me cry every time, reliving those rollercoaster feelings. But I'd done it, I'd got it, and I'd set a new Olympic record.

I got off and buried my face in Ian's neck, sobbing. Adrenalin had really kicked in now and I was shaking so badly that people kept asking me if I was all right. I was fine, but completely overwhelmed – I'd won two

Olympic gold medals. And that uproar ... when you hear it, that's a sound you will never, ever forget. The cheering and stamping and clapping were so loud you'd have thought the house was about to come down.

Laura had won the bronze, so when it came to the prize-giving there were two of us receiving medals, although this was the first time that I was stepping up on a podium on my own, without my team-mates to either side of me. Every medal is special, but an individual medal always feels a bit more special – it's a sentimental thing because it's something that you've gone out and won entirely for yourself. And did I think I deserved it? Yes, I did. I'd slightly fluffed the end, but the rest of the test had been good, and even though Blueberry was a bit tired, the picture we'd presented was still harmonious.

By this point all I wanted was to see Dean and my parents but I only had time to give them a massive hug before I was whisked straight off to do press and TV. It was the start of a whirlwind: one minute I was talking to Chris Evans, the next I was getting up at 6 a.m. for the BBC Breakfast sofa. Blueberry and I even made the front page of *The Times*.

I don't know how I came across in those interviews, but I was absolutely terrified. Life for me was going to shows, competing and coming home, job done. I'd given a few interviews after the Europeans and my world record in Hagen, but now I was being faced with a succession of people I'd never met, firing questions at me, left, right and centre. Even though they were asking me about what I'd just been doing, I'd get so nervous at the attention focused on me that I'd forget what they'd asked. I dragged Carl along when I could so that he'd be asked the questions instead, and he was very good about helping me out. But I wish I'd had some preparation and training and not just been thrown in at the deep end. Nobody had told me what it was going to be like – I felt like a rag doll, being pulled one way then the other, and each time as I stood there waiting to be interviewed, the sweat would be running down my arms and I'd be shaking with fear.

We still managed to celebrate, though. Months earlier Carl had come up with the idea of a boat trip along the Thames after the Freestyle, to mark our final night in London. The plan was that if we hadn't won gold we'd jump in and drown our sorrows, and if we had won gold, we'd party in style. We definitely managed that. The boat he had found was huge, with a dance-floor upstairs and a roof that came off so you could see the stars. It was magical, and a photographer from *Hello!* managed to get a picture of Carl, Laura and me together with Zara Tindall just as we went under Tower Bridge with its illuminated Olympic rings. Carl has helped Zara with her dressage for years, and she's brilliant fun. You might think that because she is who she is everything's easy for her, but she probably works and trains harder than anybody because of the pressure that comes from living in the limelight the whole time.

I was still being good and trying to take my role as an athlete seriously, so I only had a couple of glasses of champagne, but everyone else was, shall we say, quite tipsy by the end of that night. When heads had cleared the next morning, however, there was another challenge to negotiate: how we were all going to get home.

World Class had arranged for a people carrier to come and pick us all up from our houses for the journey down to London, but just before the Freestyle we'd learned from Dickie that we'd be expected to make our own way back. I was pretty annoyed, and I went and said as much to our World Class Performance Director

Will Connell. Travelling by train is something I hate anyway, but I couldn't believe we were being expected to take all our gear, plus our medals, home on public transport, particularly after the job we'd done.

Dickie promised to have a word with Will, but by this time, somewhat unimpressed, I'd made alternative arrangements with my sister. However Dickie kept assuring me he'd sorted something out, and the next morning what did we find but a huge white Rolls-Royce waiting for us! Now *that* was more like it! The only snag was that Will hadn't realised Ian was coming back to Gloucestershire with me and Carl, so it ended up being a bit of a squeeze with three of us and all our gear. A Rolls-Royce isn't really kitted out to deal with luggage, but hell, we were not letting that car go so we forced ourselves in.

It was the best drive home: just what we deserved. We were caught up in traffic in the Cirencester area, and Carl decided to keep everybody entertained by playing around with the blacked-out windows. He'd slowly lower them to show a fraction of his head and then, just as people were peering in hoping to get a glimpse of someone posh, slowly roll them back up again. We were all crying with laugher by the time we got home to yet more celebrations: balloons and banners all over the yard and our houses.

The horses were now due a holiday and so was everybody else. Carl had decided to celebrate his birthday by arranging a big trip to Sark and there must have been at least forty of us, including Dean, Alan, Richard Davison, Judy and Malcolm Harvey, and Trish Gardiner.

For me, it was lovely finally seeing where Carl had grown up. I'd always had a picture in my head of a breathtakingly beautiful little island where Carl had ridden his donkey and there weren't any cars, and it turned out to be pretty much exactly as I'd imagined. You and your suitcase arrive by boat, which feels quite random, and then it's a horse and cart up to the hotel. If you want to get anywhere you have to cycle, and as there are no streetlights it's like being back in olden days. One night we had to cycle back from a restaurant in the pitch black, and all you could hear was people calling, 'Where are you? Where are you?' and then falling off or riding into hedges.

We went to see Carl's gold postbox – my own had been installed back home in Gloucestershire – and the two of us gave a little talk to some the island's school kids. By now, I was even being called 'the girl on the dancing horse' in my local Tesco, although the time it struck me most was when I was in Hampshire teaching my friend, the dressage rider Alice Oppenheimer.

Whenever I'm down in Hampshire I stay at a pub owned by the family of another friend, Amy Sanders. I was in the bar one evening and three men in their late forties came over: they obviously weren't horsey, but they'd recognised me from the TV. 'We were just talking,' one of them said, 'and we want to know – are you telling that horse what to do, or is it dancing by itself?' 'Well,' I said, 'you've just made my day, because if it looks like I'm not doing anything then that's my job done.'

It was amazing to me that people who'd never had anything to do with horses, let alone dressage, were so interested in what I did. Ours isn't a sport that many people know or follow and it was fantastic to get so much publicity.

September brought the 'Our Greatest Team' Olympians parade through London. It had been arranged alphabetically, so the equestrians were on the same bus as the diving team and all I could hear were kids screaming out Tom Daley's name the whole time. The numbers of people who turned out to see and support us, I could not believe: the streets of London were absolutely rammed and there were people leaning off balconies and even standing on bins trying to get a good view. Then we went on to Buckingham Palace where there was a fly-past from the Red Arrows and speeches from Princess Anne and the Mayor of London, Boris Johnson.

Carl took the mick out of me for being a goody two-shoes and standing quietly at the front while he and Zara were being naughty at the back. Compared to him, I am a goody two-shoes, I don't deny it. He's always talking when he shouldn't be and I'm trying to be serious and listening. Being around the other athletes was so exciting but I was a bit in awe, too. As we hadn't been staying in the Olympic Village we hadn't had a chance to mix with them before, but now we were getting to see the likes of Jessica Ennis and Mo Farah. Laura and I kept nudging each other and egging each other on to ask for a picture with them, equally star-struck. 'You ask Mo!' No, *you* ask Mo!'

Then in October we were invited back to Buckingham Palace for a reception for the 2012 Olympic and Paralympic medallists. It was like being in some kind of dream, going through those famous gates and up the red carpet, and there was so much to take in – the guardsmen, the butlers, the chandeliers, the paintings. I felt like such an old person because I even found myself being impressed by the doors: I'd never seen doorframes that big and grand and ornate. 'Charlotte,' I thought, 'put your eyes back in,' because there was just so much to see and I felt like they were goggling out on stalks. Carl and I stood together in the line-up to meet the Duchess of Cambridge and she was every bit as beautiful as you'd imagine – her face, her figure. I was so envious.

She had a lovely, soft-spoken voice and she was so interested in what you had to say and made you feel like she genuinely wanted to know all about you.

The past few months had been the best, most incredible months of my entire life, but there was another side to it all that people didn't see. Just before the Olympics, the news had broken that Blueberry was up for sale. I'd always known that was Carl's plan so it didn't come as a shock, but I'd cried after every test I'd ridden at the Olympics, thinking, 'This is my last Grand Prix', and, 'This is my last Freestyle'. Part of the reason I'd been so emotional after that second gold was knowing I was going to lose him – and that was something I didn't know if I could cope with.

10

Rock Bottom

A PART OF me could, of course, understand why Carl wanted to sell Valegro. Like me Carl had to work hard for a living; he didn't have a rich family to support him, and at the end of the day he still had to pay his mortgage. Carl's Athens Olympics horse, Escapado (Peanuts), had been sold after that games, and the plan had always been to do the same with Blueberry after London.

At the time, Carl was also facing losing Uthopia. He only had a minority share in Uti, and after the Olympics life-changing amounts of money were being offered for both horses. Obviously I had been through that process myself with Fernandez, but with Blueberry it felt like a very different situation. Dez was never going to be the horse I needed him to be, and I knew in my heart of hearts that he was better off going somewhere he could be a star in his own right. With Cathrine, he was also going to have a home forever: I'd even asked her if I could have him back when he retired, but she'd told me she'd be keeping him until the day he died.

If Blueberry did have to be sold, I wasn't going to have any say in where he went, and that for me was almost the hardest thing to deal with. But I also felt that he didn't owe Carl or me anything: what he had done and what I'd achieved with him was unheard of, and he'd given so much not just to me but to the sport and to the whole country.

It was heart-wrenching and I felt trapped in the middle. I didn't want to be selfish because I knew what a difference the money would make to everyone, but at the same time I was angry with Carl. He wouldn't discuss things with me – it's never been his style and I think he probably didn't want to have to deal with my emotions. But I'm a very open person and although I have enormous respect for Carl, I felt that if we could have talked things through more, I would have been better able to cope with the situation.

Things got pretty heated and my behaviour made Carl quite cross at times, which, again, part of me could understand. But Blueberry was my partner, my best friend – my everything, really. I know there are worse things in life, but the thought that I might lose him made me feel like my heart was being ripped out and wrenched in every direction. He was a massive part of me, and the relationship I had with him was unique. Knowing that I might lose him, I really struggled to be on the yard and see him every day, and when a buyer came forward in September my parents took me to Portugal so I wouldn't have to be around. I can honestly remember nothing about it, but my mum says I was like a zombie, wandering around looking at my watch and wondering what was happening back at home.

The sale didn't go through, and with Christmas coming up, Carl was beginning to think about Olympia. He still had Uti, who hadn't yet sold, but he had decided that this would be their last show as a combination. As for me, I genuinely didn't know if I wanted to go. Since September I had been number one in the FEI world rankings, the first time that a British rider had got to the top. It was such a proud moment, and I wanted to finish my career with Blueberry at our best. If we didn't have a future, my first reaction was that I wanted to go out on the high of winning double gold at the Olympics and not risk anything going wrong. But after I'd thought about it some more, I realised that win or lose, it actually didn't matter. I'd be riding Blueberry and we'd be out there together again, and at the end of the day that was the only thing I cared about.

I usually get a cold around Olympia time and just carry on riding, but the cold I got before Olympia 2012 turned out to be bronchitis. My ears popped, my head was pounding; I rang my mum the night before the Grand Prix and she didn't believe it was me on the phone at first, I sounded so bad.

As an athlete, you have to think carefully about taking anything even if it's only Lemsip, but I went to see the team doctor who sent me off with various pills. What he didn't tell me about were all the side effects – nausea, dry mouth – so after I'd ridden and was being interviewed not only could I hardly talk, I was also ready to throw up.

Blueberry and I had managed to set a new world record in the Grand Prix, 84.447 per cent, though I'd ridden a bit more safely than I normally would have done. I now had to get myself through to the Freestyle, so the next day I stayed in bed at the Hilton Hotel, trying to get as much rest as I could. Ian sat with me, apart from when he went out to the chemist to get me some Vicks to rub on my pillow. It did the job but Ian, who was the only one who could smell it, said it made the place absolutely reek.

He has always been my shoulder to cry on, the person who picks me up and puts me in the place I mentally need to be: people often think he's my partner until I tell them that as far as Ian's concerned, I'm the wrong gender. Carl, on the other hand, is not very sympathetic if you're ill (whereas if he's ill, he's dying), and just as I was about to go into the Freestyle he scared me to death.

At the Olympics, I'd gone into the ring with a second to spare. This time Carl thought I'd actually gone over time and I could see him at the entrance, frantically telling me to hurry up and get in. I was already completely frazzled and his panic started me panicking, although I couldn't understand what was wrong: the bell had rung, I'd put my hand up and everything seemed fine. It completely threw me and I messed up the start of the test because both Blueberry and I were tense.

Most people had been expecting me to break another of Edward and Totilas's world records that night, but after everything I was just happy when we came out with 87.95 per cent. Isabell Werth got 80.075 per cent for second and Carl was third with his final ride on Uti, so it felt like a great way to end the year. But as soon as the magic Olympia bubble burst, I came smashing back to reality. On Christmas Eve, I found out that another buyer was interested in Valegro. I was also facing the end of my relationship with Dean.

* * *

After the Olympics, my life had stopped being my own. At first I was so happy and so bubbly with joy that I didn't mind, but after a while I felt I'd talked about what I'd done so much, to so many people, it had almost taken the shine off it. I had all kinds of offers of TV and media work that I turned down, which people told me I was crazy to do, but fame isn't important to me, it's not why I ride. Finding a horse that I can work with and train is what I love, more than going out and competing and trying to do well, but I was in the spotlight so much I couldn't even get on with that.

I don't want to complain because I did some amazing things after London, but it had got to the point where Dean saw more of me in the papers than he did at home. Then when I was around, everything that was happening with Blueberry meant I was probably quite difficult to be with.

On the night we were due to switch on our town's Christmas lights, Dean told me he needed to be alone to clear his head. It was horrible weather, pouring with rain, and we were trying to be cheerful and hide what was going on, but when we got home he packed his suitcases and moved out. And after that I really did hit rock bottom.

I'd always thought I was a strong person and because I was so independent, if anything happened, I'd be OK. But it's only when something's gone you really know what you've lost. I've never experienced pain like I did in those few months: it was horrendous. Ian came to stay with me but I didn't want to be at home, and when I went to stay with my mum, I didn't want to be at hers either.

Depression wasn't something I'd ever really understood before. But I'd got to the point where I was thinking about harming myself because I had no idea what to do next. It felt like I'd had everything and then it had all been taken away: I'd lost my relationship, I was going to lose my horse – my whole life had been turned upside down. Success had totally changed things for me. At that point, if I could have given my medals back and have things return to the way they were, I would have done.

Food is something I've always enjoyed but I didn't want to eat after Dean left. I lost nearly two stone, and was crying buckets: I couldn't stop. The only thing that was getting me up in the morning was riding, because when I was doing that I could shut the door on everything else. When you're with your horse, it's just the two of you together and everything else falls away. But with the uncertainty over Blueberry's future, even that felt spoiled.

Finally, at the end of January, I got a phone call from Dean. We agreed to meet to talk things through, and for the first time I understood things from his side. I'd never really thought before of what he was giving up for me, or how hard it was for him that I was always busy. When you're competing, you're here, there and everywhere, and I hadn't thought of what it felt like not to be a part of that. Realising that I hadn't been there for him when he'd always been there for me was very upsetting. A relationship works two ways, and it's sad that it took a crisis to make me appreciate that. We agreed that in future we both needed to be more open with each other about our feelings, but now, five years later, I can honestly say we're stronger than ever. We're both better at communicating and, looking back, I think that break was actually important in bringing us closer.

Meanwhile, Blueberry still hadn't sold: after everything, the potential buyers who had come forward in December had also dropped out. For the rest of the year things hung in the balance, but ultimately Carl and Roly decided they were going to keep him. They formed a syndicate and announced in the press that they were looking for investors, which is when Anne Barrott got in contact. Anne had read about what was happening in *Horse & Hound*, and when she became the third of Blueberry's owners in January 2014, we all knew he would be staying with us for the rest of his life.

Although 2012 had ended in what felt like a nightmare, it hadn't all been bad. In November I had bought a beautiful new grey mare, Florentina, together with my mum and the Dockleys. She was only two, coming up to three, and would spend another year turned away in a field at Sandra Biddlecombe's, but I already knew she was going to be a super horse.

Then, in December, I found out that I had been awarded an OBE in the New Year's Honours list. The Queen had given me my Christmas present! Although I did have to ring up my mum to ask exactly what at an OBE was – I knew it was special but I didn't realise how special until she told me.

Carl and Laura had both been made MBEs, so it was an incredibly proud moment for all of us, and for the ceremony at Buckingham Palace in January I got myself a stunning cream dress coat from Paul Costello. You know when you put something on and you feel like you've grown a couple of inches? It was that kind of outfit: you put it on and couldn't help feeling a bit important, especially if you wore horsey stuff the rest of the time. With my hair and make-up done I felt like I was ready for the races, although there you don't have to curtsey and walk out of the room backwards. My worst nightmare was that I was going to trip and fall flat on my face because it was just the kind of thing that would happen to me, but thankfully I did everything right and didn't fall over in front of Princess Anne, who was standing in for the Queen. Then my parents took Ian and me for lunch: a great end to one of the loveliest days we've all spent together.

As 2013 started, my aim was to try and move forward rather than spend time looking back. Thinking about things was just getting me down and anyway, who knew what might happen in the next year? The talk about Blueberry being sold had died down; he was still with us and I could see him every day at the yard, so that was a huge plus. And I had lots of other positive things

Carl, Blueberry and I.

Blueberry was ready for this performance. We both were.

'Holy moly!' I thought. 'I've just done the Olympics!'

The 'Our Greatest Team' Olympians parade through London. The numbers of people who turned out to support us, I could not believe!

We were invited to Buckingham Palace for a reception for the 2012 Olympic and Paralympic medallists. Carl and I stood together in the line-up to meet the Duchess of Cambridge and she was every bit as beautiful as you'd imagine.

Left: The most nerve-wracking part of receiving my MBE was my fear that I was going to trip and fall flat on my face in front of Princess Royal Anne, but thankfully I did everything right!

Blueberry and I are not machines – he can't be brilliant every time but I've been fortunate in that Blueberry always tries his best!

Having the chance to give a demonstration with the jockey A.P. McCoy was such fun. But when I was asked if he might be a Rio contender, I had to confess I thought he still had some work to do.

I was so nervous before my test in Rio but it felt like Blueberry took hold of my hand and said, 'Mum, we can do this.' And we did!

Dean is the world's best supporter, even if he did steal all the limelight with his proposal from the stand.

Bringing home a team silver at Rio was the best feeling – we'd given our all and for me it had been a pleasure to ride with every one of my team-mates.

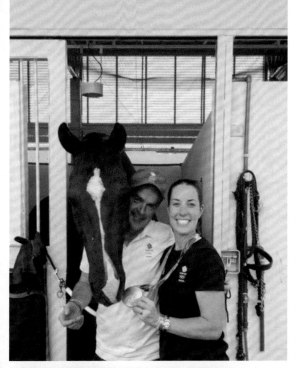

Alan Davies, our travelling groom, is definitely the key to my success – he never stresses, and he's the most incredible supporter and so proud of what our horses achieve.

Receiving a CBE for my performance at Rio was another huge honour for me.

Inset: Carl and I at the Fete Imperiale 2017 in Austria. I cannot begin to explain how much I have learnt from Carl's knowledge and experience.

With Valegro, I was able to make my very own fairytale come true. For him to finish at his best, in front of all the people who loved him, was all I could ever have wished for.

in my life and other horses that I wanted to ride – including, now, Uthopia.

With European and Olympic golds under his belt, Carl felt that he'd done everything he wanted with Uti. For me, on the other hand, the chance to ride him was an amazing opportunity to get more experience, and I already loved riding Uti at home.

We decided that I'd take him to Saumur in May, which felt like a bit of an ask: our first time competing together and we were only going to go out and do an international in front of the whole world. But in the build-up I was feeling quite cocky.

Uti isn't the easiest horse to ride and he'd got to the point with Carl where he knew the Grand Prix inside out. He'd started to get a little bit cheeky, although Carl had always done such an amazing job riding him round you'd never have known. With me, though, he was feeling super – I was even getting more lift and suspension in his trot half-passes, which he had sometimes struggled with.

'You just wait,' Carl kept saying. 'You wait.' We got to Saumur, warmed up, and Uti felt brilliant. Then as we were going round the outside and about to go into the arena, he suddenly said, 'No, thanks.'

I went down the first centre line, halted, moved off and Uti was like a snail. He did not want to go. With Blueberry, I'm thinking it and we're doing it. With Uti, I was thinking it and nothing was happening. I was kicking, I was sweating – I've never puffed so much in my life as I did trying to get him round that test. It was not something I was used to, and when I came out Carl could not stop laughing.

Uti didn't have any reason to behave that way other than the fact he was being very cheeky and idle, so I was not pleased. We won, with Carl second on Fine

Time, a ride he had taken over for Gemma Appleton, but I was determined there wasn't going to be a repeat performance in the Freestyle.

There's an old saying: 'Tell a gelding, ask a mare and discuss it with a stallion'. Uti is a stallion, but he also needed a bit of squashing down. He was trying to be a typical man and take over, and as I rode into the Freestyle I'd made up my mind he was never going to play around with me again.

I'd decided to use Blueberry's *How to Train Your Dragon* music for Uti – I thought it would suit him and I loved every minute of riding to it. I wanted to see if I could replicate on Uti a bit of the feeling I got with Blueberry, and in the end I did, but it was ten times harder. The main thing in my favour was that because Uti didn't know where he was going with my floorplan, he had to pay attention and listen to me, which meant I could school him round a bit more. It still wasn't what I wanted, and not up to Carl's standard by any means, but we came out with 81 per cent. Carl and Fine Time got 74 per cent so the two of us were first and second again, but more importantly, I was able to go home feeling that I hadn't completely failed to follow in Carl's footsteps.

With the Europeans at Herning in August now our main focus, Carl decided that I should try and qualify Uti as my second horse while he focused on Dances With Wolves (Golly).

We took them both back to France for Compiègne in June, but things didn't go to plan. I'd exercised Uti on the first day and he was fine, but then he got bitten by a fly while he wasn't wearing his rug in the stable. He'd never had a bad reaction before but flies abroad can be much bigger than the ones here, and Uti's bites were right where his saddle went.

It wouldn't have been fair to continue, but I was very disappointed to have to withdraw. The upside, however, was that it gave me more time to kick Carl's butt into shape with Golly.

Golly was a huge horse, over seventeen hands, and a very expressive mover, but he was also a real chicken. He was afraid of everything, which was a shame because he was so talented. That's the annoying thing about horses: you can have a horse with all the talent in the world, but if it doesn't have the right mentality, it doesn't matter.

At Compiègne, which doesn't have the liveliest atmosphere, Golly coped well, and Carl won both the Grand Prix and the Special. Then it was on to Rotterdam in June for Blueberry's first run of the year.

Arriving in Rotterdam, it really came home to me how much I'd achieved since I was there last. In 2011 I'd only started riding Grand Prix a few months before. I'd had three goals – to ride on a team with Carl and to compete at Olympia and the Olympics – and now, boom! I'd ticked them all off the list. More than that, Blueberry and I had broken world record after world record and I could feel that there was still more to come.

Preparation is hard when you've got a horse as good as Blueberry: you don't want to do too much and ask too much in advance, but in Rotterdam we were definitely missing the fine-tuning. In the Grand Prix, Blueberry wasn't really on my aids and had gone back to being really strong. He was also starting to question me a little, which he had never done before: going down the last centre line he got a bit sneaky and tried to stop. Most horses change when they get to their third year at Grand Prix, so it wasn't a surprise. The first year, they don't have the experience so they're relying on you as a rider. Year two, they know a bit more, your job is a bit easier, and everything is more established and polished. Year three and they really start to know the test, so then your job is to stop them anticipating and trying to take control. There isn't a horse alive that doesn't try to do it, which is fair enough: they're clever animals and just doing what we've taught them.

Although it wasn't my best test with Blueberry, 82 per cent was enough for first. As this was a Nations' Cup competition, it was also a good result for the rest of the team: Carl, Daniel Watson and Gareth Hughes. Carl finished fourth on Fine Time and Gareth came seventh, which meant we ended up beating the Netherlands and Sweden into second and third.

For the Freestyle, I'd decided to go back to *How to Train Your Dragon* – with Blueberry not at full fitness, it wasn't as demanding as my London floorplan and I wanted to give him a nice ride round. We did OK and beat Edward Gal and Undercover into second, but we'd definitely got work to do.

Uti had also come out to Rotterdam, and Carl decided I should ride him in the 3* Grand Prix and Special. We finished second to Edward in both, with Carl and Golly notching up two thirds, but by now Carl was realising that Golly just wasn't reliable enough to have on a team. However much Carl tried to give him confidence, he would still end up going into the arena and having a meltdown. There's only so much you can try and it wasn't fair on Golly because he'd get so stressed and nervous, but if he wasn't going to be coming to Herning we had a gap to fill.

I'd been encouraging Carl to get back on Uti again because I knew the team needed that boost, and after Rotterdam he agreed. The new plan was that he'd take Uti to the Europeans, and that both of us would have our final run through at Hickstead a few weeks before.

In the meantime, both horses had to be got fit without actually working them harder, which meant regular sessions on the water treadmill at Hartpury.

A lot of horses find the water treadmill quite scary because it's a narrow, enclosed space but, once again, Blueberry proved that he's a one-off. He'd get so excited each time Alan took him he'd pretty much load himself, and Alan would have to hold him back off the chest bar because his knees would come up so high out of the water. Most horses just plod through, but the movement Blueberry gets through his shoulders and back is incredible: I've been to watch him a couple of times and I love it. It's a view you never get when you're riding, and when you can see the sheets of your horse's muscles rippling and moving it's fascinating, like a living anatomy lesson.

I was feeling good going into Hickstead, but not long before Carl suggested that I change Blueberry's bit. He was getting so strong and we thought it might give me more control. Change isn't something I'm very good with and it's one area where Carl and I are quite different. I'm a great believer in leaving well alone if something's working, but Carl often likes to alter little things. Alan gets stuck in the middle sometimes, because I'm telling him one thing and Carl is telling him something else, but this time I thought I might as well give it a go because Blueberry is pretty much the same whatever bit I use.

It wasn't till I was actually at Hickstead and warming up for the Grand Prix that I realised it had been a mistake, but by that point it was too late. The thing with Blueberry is that he's never trying to be naughty; he's just so up for it all the time. He was particularly strong on the left side, and my left pirouette, which has always been my weaker of the two, was a bit of a mess. My one-time changes, which I struggled with through my entire career with Blueberry, weren't good enough either.

I was upset with myself because the changes were totally down to rider error: my legs froze up. Carl was always shouting at me about forgetting to move them – 'You have to hold him back, keep him short, use your legs' – but anyone who trains or competes knows there are a lot of things that are easier said than done. In any case, although we won both the Grand Prix and Special, we should have done much better. At the start of the Special I'd even felt we could have gone on to get another world record, but I always try and learn from mistakes and the main thing now was making sure it didn't happen again.

So Carl and I went down to Hartpury to practise my music and for the next two weeks he murdered me. My floorplan meant I had to do a line of changes to a single pirouette, then an extended canter to a double pirouette – a total of three left pirouettes. I had Ian watching and videoing me, and Trish came along as another pair of eyes on the ground, but mostly it was just Carl screaming at me and picking me up on every single little thing.

Looking back, those blips at Hickstead were the best thing that could have happened because it made me really focus and sharpen up. We ended up running through the entire test three times, which is a lot, and even when Carl was satisfied that something looked right, if it didn't feel right to me, we did it again.

By the time we'd finished it felt amazing, and I sent Carl a text afterwards to say thank you: I knew he'd appreciate it because he always likes to say he was the one who taught me manners.

The team for Herning hadn't yet been decided, but Laura and Alf had seemed a certainty. Unfortunately, Alf wasn't at his best and Laura reluctantly decided to withdraw. She was such a strong contender that it was a bit gutting, but at the same time it was good for us to have two newer riders on the team in Gareth Hughes, who Carl sometimes taught, and Michael Eilberg.

I get on really well with Michael and his dad, Ferdi, and they're both dressage fanatics. As a former top rider, Ferdi is also an incredible trainer and wants everything very correct. He's a stickler for discipline, and once Michael has ridden they'll watch his test back and go through it with a fine toothcomb. I always take the mick out of Michael because if you ask him how he's done, he'll literally take you through it step by step: 'Well, I went down the centre line, I halted, but it wasn't quite square. Then I moved off, but it wasn't quite in front of my leg; my first extension could have been better ...'

At Herning, Michael was on Half Moon Delphi, his gorgeous grey mare. He had a few blips and there was a big discrepancy in his marks, but for his team debut he did a really good job. Unfortunately Gareth, who'd been first to go, had a bit of a nightmare. His mare Nadonna couldn't cope with the atmosphere, froze, and although Gareth got her round he came out very disappointed. We tried as a team to support him because it was just one of those unfortunate things, but it meant the pressure was really on for Carl and me.

Carl rode first because he wanted to have time to help me prepare, and Uti, true to form, didn't give him the easiest ride. When he came out I'm sure he was biting his tongue, but he still got 75 per cent. Then Helen Langehanenberg went in and got 84 per cent on

Damon Hill and after that I knew it was basically down to me to get us a medal.

From the minute I got to Herning, I'd had the most amazing feeling about it. The venue was in a massive football stadium and when we'd rocked up the pitch had still been down, but just seeing it had given me a good vibe. The bigger the venue, the more I grow into it and the better I am, so I'd felt from the start that I was going to enjoy myself. This time, though, I was going to have to pull out all the stops. I knew the score I was capable of getting, but in the warm-up I could not get my ones: it was mistake, mistake, mistake, mistake. I didn't know why it was happening because Blueberry felt really good otherwise. 'Right,' I thought, 'come ON. You are going to ride every inch of this test.' I was going to go in there and I was going to nail it, and as I rode down that first line, I was on fire.

The one thing that Carl had said to me before I went in was, 'Eddie, do NOT go full pelt for that first extension.' But what was I going to do, ride for a seven or an eight? I was going out there to ride for tens, and I could hear the crowd gasping as I hit them.

For the whole test we were pretty much faultless: I was not going to give a mark away. When we came out we'd got a new world record, 85.94 per cent, and I'd also managed to get us into bronze medal position as a team.

Poor Roly turned up ten minutes too late to watch, which is so like her, but we all celebrated together – we'd only just missed out on a silver medal, and as we'd had to manage without Laura, it was an achievement for all of us.

After that, it was the Special – or 'The battle of the dumb blondes' as Carl called it. It started when the

Swedish rider Patrik Kittel made an error, and then Helen and Damon Hill went wrong too.

In the Special, you have to go down the long side at the place where, in the Grand Prix, you go across the diagonal. Unfortunately Helen set off in the wrong direction and when the bell rang and she realised what she'd done, you could see how mad with herself she was.

I'd known that Helen was the one to beat, but even though she'd had a problem I was panicking: in the warm-up my changes just weren't happening.

I remember what happened next like it was yesterday. As Carl was walking with me down through the tunnel to the arena, he said: 'You do know the test, don't you? Make sure when you come round the corner, you trot along the long side.' Fine, I thought, but we talked through the test together anyway, and for most of the time I was riding it, I was on a real high. I could hear people gasping again as we went from the passage into the extensions, but then I got into canter and went across the diagonal to do my two-times, just like in the Grand Prix. Only this wasn't the Grand Prix and I should have been doing half-passes. The bell rang and at first I was confused because I didn't know what I'd done, but then I saw the English judge, Andrew Gardner, mouthing 'HALF-PASS!' And I mouthed something I'm not going to put in print.

I was thinking that had probably put me on par with Helen, and now I couldn't make a single mistake, but as I went to pick up my test, everybody was laughing. The crowd couldn't believe Helen and I had both gone wrong, but what was funny to them was a serious distraction to me. I wanted to scream, 'Shut up!' but of course I just had to carry on and, thank the Lord, I managed to nail the rest of the test. Blueberry was foot perfect and I swear to God he must have known what we needed to do.

I came out with 85.69 per cent, 4.15 per cent more than Helen, but was that going to be enough? Carl and I were on tenterhooks. The only person who might beat me now was Adelinde, but as she was riding and I was being interviewed, I heard a commotion – she had gone wrong as well. The crowd had never seen anything like it, and when Adelinde finished on 81.54 per cent, the three of us ended up first, second and third – and yes, it was an all-blonde podium.

All that was left now was the Freestyle. I'd worked so hard with Carl at Hartpury to iron out all the creases, and to the relief of both of us it paid off. I had a tiny mistake in one of my left pirouettes – I put my leg on and Blueberry over-reacted and jumped out – but that was the only blip in the test. We almost broke Edward and Totilas's world record, but our 91.25 per cent was enough for a second gold, with Helen in silver and Adelinde in bronze.

During the prize-giving Blueberry wasn't very pleased that I wouldn't let him eat my flowers, but he got plenty of other treats. Whenever we're at a show we'll go to the supermarket and get the horses bags of carrots and apples, and they have sugar all the time. People often say that Blueberry's teeth are going to fall out with the amount of sugar he has, but I think it's important to let him know when he's done something well. I tell him he's a good boy as well, even though talking to your horse during a test isn't something you're supposed to do.

Reward is a big part of the way we work with our horses, and the aim is always to make sure that they lead a happy, healthy life. After the Olympics we were asked a lot if our horses won gold because we turned them out in the fields – well, no, there was a bit more to it than that, but they do live very normally. Lots of top dressage horses aren't turned out because of the risk that they'll hurt themselves, but Carl's philosophy and management style, which I've learned, is that horses need to be horses. It doesn't matter how precious they are, it's good for their bodies to be moving around and it's good for their brains: they need that free time just chilling out and eating grass.

It's the same when we train them. For us it's never drill, drill, drill, push, push, push. The horses we ride are athletes too, and we have to think about keeping them fit and sound long-term: you can't expect horses to last if you're pushing their bodies seven days a week. At home, our horses are schooled on Monday and Tuesday, then go hacking on Wednesday. Hacking gives them a break and a chance to think about what they've done, although it's a learning experience, too. Because Blueberry always needed to improve his walk, hill work was a great way of making him stride out, as opposed to just walk faster and faster. On Thursday and Friday it's back to schooling, by which time they'll feel like they're really on it; Saturday they go for another hack, and Sunday they have off.

We're lucky to live in a beautiful part of the country-side and there's nothing nicer than getting out in the fields, getting up off your horse's back, standing in your stirrups and going for a good old canter. The horses love it, the dogs coming hurtling round, having the time of their lives, and in summer it's like a little bit of heaven.

Rider time off is important, too. Just before Herning, Carl and I were invited to Wimbledon to enjoy a day in the Royal Box with some of the other 2012 medal-lists. I only had two tickets, and because Dean is the best, he gave up his place so that Ian could come with me. Ian eats, sleeps and breathes tennis and Carl is a massive fan, but after Beijing I wasn't really sure I was up for more.

If anywhere was going to convince me about tennis, it would be Wimbledon. The day began with a lovely lunch in the clubhouse, where all the trophies and winners' pictures are on display, then we were led out to seats that were bang on centre court and, naturally, had a perfect view. Andy Murray, Sir Chris Hoy and Victoria Pendleton were among the guests, and during the match people kept bringing us champagne and passing round a huge tub of sweets as though we were in the cinema. Then we had a break and afternoon tea with cake and scones and little special sandwiches – I can't tell you how posh we felt. As for who was playing, I can't actually remember, but having not been sure how much I was going to enjoy it at the start, it turned out to be one of the best things I've done.

Another incredible experience was being invited to ride with the Household Cavalry in Hyde Park in December. Riding in London was the weirdest experience as you had to remember to keep stopping at traffic lights, and I couldn't believe their stables, which had two storeys, a bit like a car park. I also came away feeling I'd learned so much more about the roots of dressage, which grew out of the kind of skills cavalry riders would once have needed on the battlefield.

After the Europeans, the only date left in the diary for 2013 was Olympia, and as I went into it there was one thing on my mind: that last world record. Edward and Totilas had set the Freestyle record, 92.30 per cent, at Olympia in 2009, and I'd been so close to breaking it at Herning. I was desperate to get the hat-trick and, having had that glimpse, I thought this time I might be able to do it – although anything could still happen on the night.

First there was the Grand Prix, and as I hadn't been out on Blueberry in four months, I wanted to use it as a schooling round for him. We had a mistake at the start of our canter work, but still managed to beat Edward, who was riding Undercover, into second.

Every time I watch Edward, he blows me away: he's a genius at zigzags, he's a genius at pirouettes, and I knew breaking the record he'd set was going to be incredibly tough. Watching him with Totilas was something else; the two of them had set a standard in dressage that had never been witnessed before. Blueberry was often called 'The new Totilas', but to me it had never been a case of one horse being better than the other – I saw it more as a baton that had been passed on. Valegro and Totilas were two different horses, but both phenomenal, and for people to have seen two such special horses at the top was something I thought was great for the sport and the spirit of dressage, whether you were competing or just watching at home.

I'd already decided that Olympia was going to be my last time riding to my London 2012 music: it seemed right to retire it in London, in front of a home crowd, and with that magical Olympia atmosphere.

The Grand Prix result had given me a boost, but this was one test where I didn't want there to be a single mistake. I wanted to get everything right for that final ride – and I did. I sometimes struggled with my music because I'd feel a bit behind it: I'd be chasing to keep up, and then because I'd be rushing we'd have a mistake. This time, I was bang on it: everything happened on the beat; I got every single pirouette; I got every single change; I did everything I knew I needed to. After I'd got past the left pirouette, the pirouette that I'd had a problem with at Herning, I could breathe again, and from then on it felt like the ride of my life. I finished, came out, and I heard the crowd go crazy: we'd got 93.975 per cent.

After the year I'd had, never knowing what was going to happen with Blueberry, it felt like the ultimate fairytale. Last year had been mind-blowing and I'd thought after that things couldn't get any better, but now here I was. There were tears rolling down my face as I rode out.

Edward and Undercover were second, and afterwards I went over to apologise to him for breaking the last of his records. I didn't want him to think I was gloating, but he gave me a hug and congratulated me, which, coming from him, meant a huge amount. Now I had all three world records the press wanted to know what I was going to do next, and I told them I had the 2014 Worlds in my sights: I'd done the Europeans, I'd done the Olympics; only the Worlds were missing. But that night all I really wanted to concentrate on was enjoying the moment – I was so grateful to Carl and Roly and Anne, and knowing that I was going to be able to continue riding Blueberry made me feel like the luckiest girl alive.

11

On Top of the World

I FINISHED 2013 on top of the world: number one in the world rankings; the holder of all three world records and, to top it all, the recipient of the FEI Athlete of the Year Award.

The FEI ceremony was held in Montreux in November, and the fashion designer Reem Acra kindly offered to lend me a dress for the occasion. Reem is the sponsor of the FEI World Cup Dressage series and has designed gowns for everyone from Melania Trump to Madonna; the silver ballgown she chose for me was one I found out later Angelina Jolie had wanted to wear, which was a real holy moly moment.

Unfortunately, when it arrived it didn't quite fit, so I nipped round to the lady who makes my curtains and got her to shorten the shoulders. Only when I arrived in Switzerland and it still wasn't sitting right did I think of ringing the Reem Acra office, and obviously not only did they know exactly what to do, they flew two girls all the way out to Switzerland just to do it.

It turned out what I needed was 'tit tape' – apparently it's what the catwalk models use all the time. You're literally stuck into your dress with double-sided sticky tape so you don't accidentally flash people, then you're good to go.

The triple-jumper Jonathan Edwards presented me with my award, and when the house band made the mistake of leaving their guitars while they took a break,

Jonathan and I couldn't resist jumping on stage and having a strum. (We got told off afterwards, but it was worth it.) As for the view of Lake Geneva that Dean and I found when we opened our hotel room curtains the next morning – it's moments like those when I really do feel like I'm living the dream.

From top of the world it was then down under. The eventer Greg Smith had gone back to live in New Zealand since his days as Carl's stunt dummy, and had often told me to come and visit. The idea of twenty-four hours on a plane really didn't appeal, but bless Greg, he wouldn't give up, so we planned a trip for the start of January 2014. It wasn't ideal timing-wise because I'd be coming back, jet-lagged, with less than a week before the World Cup qualifier in Amsterdam, but I knew Blueberry would be in good hands with Carl while I was away.

Greg set up some teaching for me in Auckland, but he also wanted Dean and me to experience as much of New Zealand as possible. We went for some fabulous drives together through scenery you wouldn't believe existed until you saw it for yourself: mountains, glaciers, and – the highlight for me – Lake Tekapo in the South Island, with water a turquoise colour that's out of this world. Of course, we couldn't go to New Zealand without trying a bungee jump. I'm glad I did it, because the part where I found myself swinging slowly upside down over a river was quite nice. But I don't think I'd do it again.

Dean's ambition for the trip was to find a beautiful beach and go for a gallop, which sounded fine, but I knew what his riding was like. He couldn't ride at all when I met him so I'd taught him the basics, but gallop? On the beach? I didn't think so. Fortunately Greg managed to find a horse he thought Dean would be safe on and we all ended up having a good old gallop in the waves. Almost as much fun was watching Dean try to walk the next day: his legs were killing him. Dean likes to tease me by saying I sit down all day doing nothing, so as far as I was concerned it was complete and utter payback.

* * *

The one thing I knew Carl was going to find tricky on Blueberry while I was away were his changes. Because Carl is so tall he rides with his stirrups six holes longer than I do, so when he asks for a change his leg is in a completely different position.

We all have our own way of riding the advanced moves, which is another reason why I'd never want to buy a ready-made horse. Everything is very personalised at the top level, and so Carl will sometimes struggle to do things on my horses and I'll struggle with his. Normally, he can teach any horse to do anything, but he never did manage to master ones on Blueberry, which, because it's probably the only thing I have over Carl, I loved.

The day I got back from New Zealand I got on Blueberry and we did a line of ones. They were perfect, but I was a long way short of my best. When it came to Amsterdam, I felt rotten with jet-lag and rusty in the arena, and in the Grand Prix there were several 'pat the horse, slap the rider' moments. The Freestyle the next day was much, much better – I'd decided to use the very first music that Tom had made for me so I knew I could just relax and have fun. The only real blip was when a camera flash went off while we were in canter: I missed a change because of it, and I had a few words with the photographer when I came out. But with just over 91 per cent it was two wins out of two, and I'd done what I'd needed to reach the final in Lyon in April.

* * *

I know what Blueberry means to me, so I can understand that for some people meeting him is a dream come true. The *X-Factor* winner Leona Lewis is a great horse lover and so when she said she wanted to come and visit the yard for her birthday in April we were delighted to say yes. We gave her a little go on Blueberry and she enjoyed it so much that we invited her to the World Cup Finals, hardly expecting she'd have the time to come, but she jumped at the chance. To have her there and to ride in front of her, knowing the kind of schedule she has and the effort she'd made to be there, was lovely.

There's no rule in dressage that says you have to keep changing your Freestyle floorplan: some riders use the same ones for years and only change their music. With so many tests to remember already I can see the attraction, but I like to keep things fresh and challenge myself. For the World Cup Final I really wanted to up my game, and as Carl is brilliant at designing Freestyles, we decided to sit down together and come up with something new.

The degree of difficulty in my London test was already quite high, but Blueberry was a year older and I was a year more experienced. Carl had always had an idea for a sequence that began with a passage half-pass to the right, into a piaffe half-pirouette turning to the right, then a passage half-pass to the left, and finally a trot half-pass to the right. If it sounds a lot written down, imagine trying to ride it. Carl told me what he was thinking, and I said: 'I'm going to do *what*?' I thought he was joking at first. When I started trying to ride it, it felt ridiculously hard, but of course, that was the point. Then we moved all my changes on to curved lines, so from start to finish it was a test that allowed absolutely no room for error.

I had enough time practising at home to feel quite comfortable with it, but I knew it was going to be another thing pulling it off in the arena at Lyon. And – story of my life – I still didn't have any music.

I'd asked Tom Hunt to come up with a different arrangement of *How To Train Your Dragon,* but it wasn't until the day before the final that he emailed it through. Then when I had a sound check, it was so distorted I had to get him to send another link urgently. That's when I did have heart failure. By the time I went in, all I was hoping was that I'd start and stop when my music started and stopped, but working with Carl has helped me learn to keep my cool whatever is thrown at me, and it always seems to be that the more pressure I'm under, the better I ride. Whatever the secret, we won with 92.17 per cent. Helen and Damon Hill were second; Edward and Undercover were third, and I was now holder of three of the four major titles: European, Olympic and World Cup. Only the World Equestrian Games title was missing, and they were coming up in August in Normandy, but before that I had Aachen in July to prepare for. And before that, I had a date with the Queen.

* * *

When I'd got back from New Zealand, I'd found a message on my phone from Buckingham Palace, asking me to ring back. I thought at first I must have done something wrong when I went to collect my OBE, although it seemed a bit strange.

It turned out the Queen wanted to invite me to a private lunch, and was I free on 8 May? I'm embarrassed to say that at first I said I was going to have to check my diary – blame the jet-lag – before reality hit me.

'I didn't mean it like that ... honestly!'

I'd have cancelled anything to be there.

I tried to find out who else had been invited, but the whole thing was top secret. The list of guests came through the day before and instead of the crowd I'd been expecting there were only ten or twelve other people and I had no idea who any of them were. I wasn't allowed to take anyone with me, which for me was a really scary prospect, and I was so worried about being late that I made Dean get up at the crack of dawn to drive me down to London.

We arrived with hours to spare so were driving up and down the Mall most of the morning to kill time. How we didn't get arrested I don't know, because we were acting like a couple of very dodgy characters.

Finally, the moment arrived and off I trotted. When you visit Buckingham Palace, after your coat has been taken, the first thing that happens is you get told where the lavatories are. As I'd been through this twice before I was able to thank the gentleman usher and tell him I already knew my way around, actually, which I think he found quite funny.

After that we were taken to a beautiful dining room and, let me tell you, I have never seen so much cutlery in my life. There was masses of it to either side of every plate. I had no clue what I was going to do with it, but the man sitting next to me turned out to be the Lord Chamberlain, the Rt. Hon. the Earl Peel. He'd obviously researched me, as he must do all of Her Majesty's guests, and he soon put me at ease.

By the time we'd had two courses I'd totally relaxed, so when the servers started bringing in lovely cut-glass bowls full of water I was a bit thrown: were they decorations? Did you drink out of them? 'Watch what Her Majesty does,' my new best friend Earl Peel advised – it turned out they were finger bowls to go with our fruit.

Afterwards we were taken to a drawing room to have tea and I was just talking to a lady who'd introduced herself as the cook Lorraine Pascale when Her Majesty came over. 'Breathe! Breathe! Breathe!' I kept thinking to myself, because it was *only the Queen* standing next to me. Her Majesty talked to Lorraine and another guest for a few moments, then she turned round and said: 'Now: you've never seen anybody ride like this young lady here.'

I couldn't believe it. I'd just received a compliment *from the Queen*! We then talked about Windsor, because I was going to be riding Uti there later in the month and Her Majesty had show horses competing. She was so knowledgeable and warm that I completely forgot who I was talking to – which you're probably not meant to do when it's HM – and when I did finally go home I was buzzing like a kid. What a huge honour.

* * *

Windsor was a nice outing for both Carl and me. Uthopia let me help him in the Grand Prix, which we won, and Carl was third on his new horse, Nip Tuck (Barney), who at eighteen hands was even bigger than Golly. We ended up in the same positions for the Freestyle, and I really couldn't have asked for more from Uti.

By now, I'd been on such a high, for so long, that I was bound to have a fall. But knowing that didn't make it any less tough.

Aachen has never been Carl's favourite venue: being in Germany feels like entering the lion's den anyway, and at Aachen the atmosphere is incredibly intense. In England you don't often get big crowds at equestrian events, and when you do they're mostly ladies with the odd man. The men are usually husbands who don't know much about dressage, but in Aachen there are thousands of men, many of them farmers, and all of them really into their horses.

It's a crowd full of people who know exactly what they're looking at, and naturally all of them are rooting for the German combinations. But the problem for me in 2014 wasn't the intimidating atmosphere so much as the weather.

We all knew that Blueberry didn't like heat, but the weather when we arrived in Aachen was so hot and humid even I didn't want to be outdoors. What was worse was that the sun was reflecting off the white sand of the arena: it was so bright you could hardly see. The Grand Prix was on the Thursday and I began warming Blueberry up in the cool of the indoor school before taking him outside for the last fifteen minutes. Already I could tell something was wrong – he felt flat and not himself at all – and when we went into the arena it was an absolute disaster. For the first time Blueberry went badly and for the first time I hated every minute of what I was doing. I messed up my twos, my piaffe and passage just weren't good enough, and we were both suffering in the heat. The press speculated that I might have been feeling the pressure of competing against Totilas, who was just coming back after a long time off through injury. But I'd competed against him in the past, and at the end of the day who I'm up against is irrelevant to me: I can't change it, so I don't worry about it. Blueberry wasn't at full fitness, true, but that was a decision Carl and I had taken as we didn't want to peak before the Worlds, and ultimately Aachen was only prep. But in the end that slight lack of fitness combined with the heat and humidity was enough for the wheels to come off, and when I came out I really felt I had zero confidence.

We ended up sixth with 76.90 per cent. Matthias and Totilas won with 82.30 per cent; Helen and Damon Hill were second, and Adelinde and Parzival were third. It was a situation I'd never been in before with Blueberry, and although Carl was supportive it was a shock to both of us. Blueberry and I are not machines, but we'd been performing so consistently that to finish unplaced was a real blow: we hadn't lost like that in over two years.

Afterwards, I locked myself in the lorry with Ian so that no one could come and speak to me. I knew everybody would want to hound me – asking what had gone wrong and how I could fix it – and I could imagine what was going to be written on social media.

Reading comments on the internet is something I've always avoided because I know how vicious people can be. Often they want to take pictures and write about their favourite riders for positive reasons, but there are a handful who say horrible, spiteful things. Riders can end up being portrayed as monsters, which I find deeply upsetting – I know my horses and Carl's are happy in what they do and that as riders we love them to bits. Ours is a sport where people are always looking to secure a psychological edge, so not getting drawn into knocking games is important: it's why I prefer to keep myself to myself at shows. But, on the other hand, you can't just hide away when it goes wrong.

I threw myself down on the sofa in the lorry, running with sweat, and tried to cool down. 'I can't even think about the Special,' I said to Ian. 'I can't go out there.' If I could have arranged not to go back into that arena, I would have. The vibe had been horrible and I really didn't think I could go through it again, but of course you can't withdraw because you haven't performed well; besides, I didn't want to be a bad sport. I had to suck it up, move on and do better, but for the first time I felt afraid. I was afraid of getting it wrong, I was afraid of making mistakes and I was afraid of being criticised by people. These were emotions I'd never experienced before when I was competing and I felt completely out of my depth.

The Special was on the Saturday, and as I rode into the arena I had tears in my eyes: the fear was awful. 'You'll be fine, Eddie,' Carl kept saying, but the soundtrack in my head telling me I couldn't do it was drowning him out.

We did better this time, second only to Mathias and Totilas, which gave me a bit more confidence, although I still messed up my changes. Then I had to go back out fighting again for the Freestyle. I'd kept away from the media because I didn't want anything to put me off, and this time our 87.90 per cent was enough to win, with Helen second and Isabell Werth on her new horse, Bella Rose, third. (Mathias had made the decision to withdraw Totilas.)

Nevertheless, I went home shaken. Blueberry hadn't been at the top of his game, but normally when he didn't give his best, it was still enough. He couldn't be brilliant every time but I'd been fortunate in never having a bad ride until now and knew I was going to need some help picking myself up again.

It was thanks to World Class that I found the sports psychologist Kate Goodger. Sports psychology had been a huge help at the start of my career, and the first time that Kate and I sat down together, she had me to a tee within seconds. I'm not easily impressed by people, but Kate worked me out so quickly it nearly reduced me to tears. What she realised was that it wasn't the pressure of performing that I needed help with – my 'same old stuff, just a different arena' attitude quite impressed her. It was the way the media fed into my own doubts that was the problem, and how I struggled with the inner voice I'd always had that told me I couldn't do things.

Kate works via the Chimp Management system. The idea of Chimp Management started with a British psychiatrist, Dr Steven Peters, who began helping the British cycling team in 2001. In 2012 he wrote a book, *The Chimp Paradox*, explaining that your brain is divided into three. There's a human part, which is rational; a chimp part, which is irrational and driven by emotions; and a computer, which handles memory. There are also gremlins, which are the negative beliefs that get in the way of what you want to do.

After I started seeing Kate, she'd come to my house and I'd sit at the kitchen table with her, ranting and raving. Then suddenly she'd say, 'Charlotte, who's talking? Is it your human? Or is it your chimp?' and it would stop me dead in my tracks.

I know I may not come across as an emotional person: I'm quite tough, as you have to be to work in my sport and the equine industry as a whole. I'm blunt and I can be outspoken, but if I don't stand up for myself, nobody else is going to do it for me. People don't always understand the time and effort that goes into training horses, and almost all riders have had the experience of rides being taken away from them. It had happened to me so much as a kid that after nearly losing Blueberry in 2012 I'd decided my days of getting on anything were over. I didn't want to be in the same situation of power-lessness again, and now I only train and compete horses that I have at least a 50 per cent share in.

But there's another side of me that's quite vulnerable. I take things to heart, I get hurt, and then I start to doubt myself.

My chimp, the part of me that tells me I'm not going to be able to do things, I decided to call Betty. Kate helped me realise that when I got stuck in a negative rut it was often Betty that was behind it, and this was the first step in being able to take charge of my fears and self-doubt.

The difference it made was tremendous. After London, when I'd been thrown in at the deep end, I'd panic every time I saw a TV camera. I'd sweat and be terrified I wouldn't know what to say. What Kate helped me realise was that the journalists weren't out to get me, they were simply doing their job. My fear of them was only a gremlin trying to take over, and I could learn to put it in a box at the back of my mind. The more I broke down my fear of the media and realised that they weren't scary people, just people asking me questions about my passion, the better at interviews I became.

It was Kate who really taught me to transform my way of thinking and turn negatives into positives. Yes, Germany had been a horrible experience, but in the long run it only made me stronger, and with the World Equestrian Games ahead I was ready to go back out and fight.

The World Equestrian Games are held every four years and bring together all the equestrian disciplines: not just dressage, showjumping and eventing but sports like vaulting and endurance riding as well.

I'd had a little taste of what a Games was like when I'd gone out to Kentucky in 2010 to support Carl and the rest of the British team. It was by far the biggest competition I'd seen at that point; the crowds were ginormous, and the atmosphere for the Freestyles – which were held at night under floodlights – was sensational.

In Normandy, there was a huge field of one hundred horses for the Grand Prix, which would decide the team competition. Michael and Gareth would be riding Delphi and Nadonna as they had at the Europeans, but Carl had decided to bring Barney: even though he lacked experience, he was more reliable than Uti or Golly.

All of us were worried by the state of the warm-up arenas, which were sand instead of the waxed surfaces we have at home and much less cushioned: you could hear the thuds of your horses' hooves. The facilities for spectators were also horrendous, and on the first day of the Grand Prix poor Carl had to do battle with the weather. As usual, he did an incredible job despite having to slosh round, and it was obvious from his 74 per cent score that he and Barney were an improving combination. Gareth also did well on day one, but the second day didn't get off to a great start for Michael and Delphi and I knew I'd have to get a high 80 per cent if we were going to medal.

The rain had held off for my test, but as I rode in the skies were black. With such a lot resting on my performance, and not having competed since Aachen, I'm sure people thought that I would fall to pieces, but I was there to prove them wrong. I'd learned so much in the months since that I knew what had happened there was never going to happen again. Fitness-wise,

Blueberry had peaked, and mentally I couldn't be more ready and up for it.

Normandy was another stadium where noise carries, and again I could hear gasps as I was riding, but whereas in the past I would have automatically thought it was because I'd done something wrong, this time I knew it was because of the tens flashing up on the board.

Coming out with 85.27 per cent, I felt as proud as punch. The German team were on amazing form but I'd lifted us into silver medal position ahead of the Dutch, and after all one hundred horses had gone Blueberry and I were still on top as the first-placed combination.

The Special I knew would be tough, with Helen and Damon Hill breathing down my neck, but Blueberry was feeling great and I thought I'd put my foot down in the Ferrari.

The one thing I hadn't planned on was that he would need to go to the toilet, but unluckily that was exactly what happened when I asked for the transition from collected walk to piaffe. 'Jesus, Blueberry!' I thought. 'Right at the wrong moment!' But what can you do? When you've got to go you've got to go.

We had another hiccup in our twos, which was pure rider error, but 86.12 per cent was enough for our second gold. We were also given a standing ovation, which is always a lovely moment when you know people have seen and appreciated your hard work.

That just left the Freestyle, where we managed a score that was only 1.8 per cent short of our world record. More than that, Blueberry and I had now equalled Anky van Grunsven and Salinero's grand slam: in the 1990s they had been the first-ever combination to be simultaneous World, Olympic and European champions, as well as Aachen Grand champions and the holders of the World

Cup. The only sadness for me was that as I climbed onto the podium to have the gold medal hung round my neck, my mum and dad weren't there to see it.

My parents had both come out to France, but official accreditation was limited. With Ian and Dean both needing passes, I didn't have enough for my mum as well, which was disappointing for her. My dad was caught in the middle, and there was a heated conversation. They watched my first two tests, then decided to pack and go home.

My parents' support means the world to me but our relationship – like any other – has its ups and downs. To begin with I found that upsetting but, again, Kate helped me with my thinking. Now if my parents come to watch me, it's fantastic, and if they decide not to I know they'll still be supporting me and watching at home.

Learning that I couldn't change people, only my own reaction to them, was a revelation for me. It also transformed my working relationships: I'm a little bit OCD and so I hate altering plans once they're made, whereas Carl's way of working is to keep things much more fluid. In the past that's caused tension between us, but Kate helped me realise that not everyone is like me and I need to accept people for who they are.

I can read people now in a way that I couldn't before working with her, which is particularly interesting at competitions. I'll watch other riders getting stressed and nervous and see how their chimp is taking over, and it's fascinating knowing why they're acting as they are. I've even recommended Chimp Management to several of my dressage rider clients, and we talk and laugh about our chimps together – it sounds completely crazy, but it really has changed my life.

* * *

Equitana is an international trade fair for equestrian sports, and in November 2014 the Melbourne event attracted 50,000 visitors over four days. I'd been invited to give a couple of demonstrations and had asked Judy Harvey to come out there with me for moral support – even with Kate's help, I still found the thought of speaking in front of hundreds of people intimidating.

I had not been to Australia before, but by now I'd learned something about long-haul travel. Judy and I were lucky enough to be flying business class and as soon as we'd taken off, I excused myself and went and got changed into my pink pyjamas. I received a few odd looks – from Judy, as well – but if you're going to be stuck on a plane for twenty-four hours, you might as well feel at home, mightn't you?

As for jet-lag, we knew going to bed when we arrived was a bad idea, so we'd barely touched down before we were off on a horseback vineyard tour. Wine isn't my thing, but the scenery was beautiful and after so long riding Blueberry I thought this was my chance to have a go on something that was the complete opposite. I wanted the biggest, clumsiest, hairiest horse I could find, which turned out to be a part-Clydesdale with mane everywhere and feet like dinner plates. Usually, we worry about the effect the ground is going to have on our horses' legs; this time, it was the other way round. When I asked him to canter he got the surprise of his life: I don't think he'd ever had to go faster than a walk before.

We were given the full VIP treatment, including a trip to Sydney and a behind-the-scenes visit to the zoo there. But it was still a working holiday, and the point of my visit was to perform Blueberry's *How to Train Your Dragon* Freestyle, with the twist that I'd be on a completely strange horse.

I got to sit on it just three times before our demonstration, and I had do some quick thinking to adapt the routine: he was being ridden in a much longer, flatter outline than I was used to, as well being very green at Grand Prix. Need I say it wasn't my greatest ride, but I think everyone had fun and I got away with skipping my final piaffe pirouette.

While I was in Australia, a phone call came through to say that I'd won the *Sunday Times* and Sky Sports Sportswoman of the Year Award 2014. To be recognised like that was quite an emotional experience for me, and it was also emotional accepting my award by live video-link: thinking of everyone in the TV studio back in the UK made me feel pretty homesick. Unfortunately in Melbourne it was blowing a gale, so while everyone back at home was all dressed up, I had to make my speech standing on a patch of scrubland watching wheelie bins rolling around in the wind. Honestly, the glamour.

Winning the BT Sport Action Woman of the Year 2014 and being nominated for the BBC Sports Personality of the Year were two more huge and unexpected honours. Dean, Ian and my friend Franky and I flew up to Glasgow for the Sports Personality ceremony in December, where this time I was fortunate enough to be wearing a dress designed by Jenny Packham. I felt like a million dollars, but when I walked into the packed SSE Hydro auditorium I wished I were a horse who could just nap and bolt out. Was I really about to stand on stage, in front of all those people, and be interviewed by Clare Balding? 'Just please don't embarrass yourself, Charlotte,' I kept thinking.

Lewis Hamilton, who had recently won his second Formula One World Title, went away with the award on the night, but it was an incredible moment for me and our sport to come fourth with 75,815 votes. Then, with Olympia starting the next day, it was straight back on the plane and down to London.

I don't think if I'd planned it, my preparation could have gone better. Compared to standing in front of everyone in Glasgow, knowing the millions of people who had been watching at home, anything else felt like it was going to be easy. Or it did until I realised I'd forgotten my lucky breeches.

After winning my world record in Hagen, I'd taken off the breeches I'd been wearing and written 'World Record' on the label so I'd always remember which ones they were. Clearly they were lucky, although I decided I could only wear them with Blueberry because otherwise they'd have got worn out with all the washing. When I got to my hotel in London, however, I found out I'd forgotten to pack them. I had to quickly go and buy another pair from one of the trade stands but it turns out it couldn't have been down to my clothing after all, because Blueberry and I still managed to break both our Grand Prix and Freestyle world records.

Marks for the Freestyle are divided between artistic and technical, and in the artistic Blueberry came away with a mark of 99 per cent. It was so close, we just needed one little thing, but whenever you ride to music some judges might like what you're doing and give you a ten, and some might be less keen and give you an eight or nine: that's just our sport. In any case, when I'm riding percentages never even cross my mind: what matters to me is what it's feeling like at the time.

Technically, I knew Blueberry would never score 100 per cent because he had never had a walk for a ten. Even a ten doesn't mean perfect – nine is defined as 'very good' and ten is 'excellent'. Judges can also only mark what they see on the day, whereas if I've done all that I can, and my horse has done all it can, what anybody else thinks isn't really that important to me. Sometimes I'll be on form and my horse will have a blip, and sometimes I'll feel as though I've let my horse down, so the goal is always for the two of us to be in harmony.

With Blueberry, it would often happen that I'd made a mistake with one thing in one test, which I'd fix, and then have a problem with something else in our next test. To be fault-free in everything took years and years, which is why we kept getting stronger and stronger as a combination. As time went on we kept climbing and climbing, so that the last few tests we rode together were pure pleasure for me: everything flowed, there was nothing more I could do and Blueberry had given his all. And that, for me, is what perfection is.

12

The Horse of a Lifetime

HOW MUCH IT meant to people to see me and Blueberry came home to me in April 2015. We were in Las Vegas for the World Cup Final, and I was taking time off to do signings for two of my sponsors, Kingsland and Equipe.

The first signing was an early morning one and I hadn't thought anyone would turn up, but when I got to the stand there was already a long queue. I was nowhere near finishing by the time I had to go to the next signing, so I told everyone waiting to come over with me, only to find a second queue so long I couldn't see the end of it.

Occasions like these are surreal for me: incredible, but strange. I don't see myself as anyone special or famous, I'm just lucky to do what I love doing, but people tell me I've inspired them and I'm their hero. I feel very honoured that I have such support, but it's also a little bit weird: people want to hug you, people want to touch you, people want to kiss you – you feel almost like a puppet. 'I'm a normal human being,' I want to say, 'I'm just me,' but it's amazing and humbling to have people so overwhelmed by emotion that they start crying when they meet you. I always have to ask them if it's because they're happy.

As for Vegas itself, who in the world would have thought of having a horse show there? I was looking out of the aeroplane window as we were flying in to land and everything was brown – there wasn't a blade of grass in sight.

Had I not been competing, it's a place I would never have visited, but what a brilliant opportunity this was. All the riders were staying in the MGM Grand, the entire bottom floor of which is a casino, and when I got up early to go out and ride Blueberry, I'd see people at the tables who'd been there when I went to bed the night before.

People gamble in Vegas morning, noon and night – it's another world. We wanted to have a good look around so we went into all the hotels including the Venetian, which is nuts – like a miniature Venice with gondoliers and canals. We managed trips to the Cirque du Soleil and a Michael Jackson tribute show where Michael Jackson appeared as a hologram, and I ended up having my picture taken with an Elvis impersonator. What a job to have, standing by the Vegas sign all day with a troop of feather-wearing showgirls – and the best part was that every time Elvis got paid, he'd roll his trouser leg up and shove the wedge of cash down his sock.

It was a crazy place and it seemed almost as crazy that we'd flown Blueberry all the way out there just for a few days. He's usually a good traveller – but, unfortunately, not this time.

The year had begun for us in January in Amsterdam, when Blueberry had won both the Grand Prix and Freestyle. I'd just come back from teaching in New Zealand so was feeling seriously jet-lagged and not at all pleased with the way I rode, but Blueberry was his usual amazing self, and in the Freestyle we finished with 93.90 per cent, 11 per cent ahead of Daniëlle Heijkoop in second.

The difference between our English winter and the 30-degree heat of Nevada hit Blueberry hard, though.

Alan had flown out with him a few days earlier. When I arrived and went to the stables to see Blueberry I wanted to cry: he's normally so lively and energetic, but now his eyes were dull and he looked very unwell in himself. We had a travelling vet with us who hooked up a drip straight away, then Alan took over and stayed with Blueberry in his stable for as long as regulations allowed. Horses have never been a nine-to-five job for Alan, which is why we're so lucky to have him.

After that Blueberry picked up and acclimatised well, but in the warm-up arena, which wasn't air-conditioned, he still felt a little bit tired. Yet as soon as we were in the cool of the stadium, he came alive. The trophy was on display under a spotlight at the edge of the arena and a lot of horses were spooking at it, but I'm sure Blueberry only had his eye on it because he was thinking about winning it.

It's that mentality that makes him unique: he's a horse who just loves performing. He'd stand on a stage all day long if he were a human celebrity, and yet the funny thing is you could drive past him on the road at home in Gloucestershire and think he was just a happy hacker, he's so chilled as he ambles along.

I had wondered if Blueberry would be nervous of the applause in Vegas, because there were 11,000 people crammed into the Thomas & Mack Centre. The arena only just fitted in, and the judges had to sit at one end in a special recessed alcove as there was so little space. But as usual, Blueberry was lapping up the attention.

Riding down that last centre line of the Freestyle was one of those moments when you feel something has just happened that will never be surpassed: I knew as I did it that this was the horse of a lifetime I was on. We got 94.196 per cent, including forty-one tens, beating

Edward and Undercover by 9.5 per cent; we'd also pipped them in the Grand Prix by 6.4 per cent. Afterwards, Edward joked that 'ninety is the new eighty'; before he had come along with Totilas, even seventy-something had seemed like a good score. But in the years since then the quality of horses and the standard of riding had gone up and up and up, and in response the judges had finally started to get brave enough to come out and give tens.

Our title defended, it was going to be a quiet year for Blueberry: the Europeans at Aachen in August were the main aim. For me, it was non-stop. I'd barely got back from Las Vegas before I was off to give a clinic in Canada.

Teaching has taken me all round the world and it's something I love doing. I don't beat around the bush: if you've come for a lesson, you've got to be open to criticism. But I love trying to encourage people to be better and give them the determination and confidence to do things they think they can't do. When something clicks with someone and they get a massive smile on their face, or when they text me to tell me they've just won, that feels as good as if I've just won myself. I try to make it fun as well (another thing I've learned from Carl, who's always cracking jokes and taking the mick). If all you did was stand there, droning on, it would bore everyone senseless. I'm the first to admit that I'd never be a dressage judge – I'd never have the patience to sit there all day – so I always try and entertain people as well as help them learn.

With the amount of travelling, teaching and competing I do, my life would be impossible without my manager, Abby Newell, and Carl's PA, Claudine Bichard.

I'd initially had organisational help from Julia Hornig, my then sponsor at Classic Dressage, but there was a lot that my mum and I were trying to deal with ourselves. When Abby came on board, everything changed: she's ruthlessly efficient and has incredible business sense. It wasn't until I started working with her that I realised having two gold medals meant I was probably worth more than I thought I was. Abby is also the one who does all my emails, which means I dread answering her calls because even if I beg her to let me off I know she'll make me sit down and go through them with her.

Things wouldn't run the way they do either without Claude, who handles all the competition entries for me and Carl. Sometimes I don't know how she has any hair left between the two of us: she always makes sure we're entered for shows by the closing date, whereas if I'm left to myself I normally forget and end up having to do it on the day.

With Blueberry having a quieter year, 2015 was a chance for me to branch out. In July, I was lucky to have the chance to perform a pas-de-deux with Isabell Werth, which was organised by the Mannheim Riding Club to celebrate the one hundredth anniversary of the Mannheim Nations' Cup showjumping competition.

Everything that Isabell does is accomplished with incredible military precision, so by the time we'd walked through the floorplan with her telling me what to do Every. Single. Step. of the way, I felt like a Churchill dog, I was nodding so much.

The challenge of pas-de-deux – besides not riding into each other – is keeping in time with your partner. If you make a mistake, you need to think quickly to catch up with them. The horse I'd kindly been lent didn't have the Grand Prix experience of Isabell's horse so the handling wasn't the easiest, but Isabell was great fun and a good laugh to work with, and it was an enjoyable night.

This year also saw a chance for my younger horses to step forward and for another partnership, this time a human one, to take off.

I've known Emma Blundell since my showing days, and she has always been a great supporter of me and Valegro: at every competition Emma is always the first to buy a bottle of champagne and crack it open. She competes herself, but in 2013 had decided to use her masters in business administration to found the Mount St John Equestrian stud at her home in Yorkshire. Her plan was to use IVF techniques to breed horses with top-level dressage potential, and as her programme progressed she asked me if I'd be interested in riding for her.

The first dressage horse that Emma bought was Freestyle, a five-year-old German mare. Emma sent me a video of her initially because she wasn't sure if she'd be good enough for me. When I finally sat on her, her paces felt very normal, but she had a look on her face that I just fell in love with: massive eyes that looked like she was wearing eyeliner and big, floppy ears. Being young, she was still quite weak when I started training her, but I could already feel there was something in there, and after a few months I knew she was going to be a special horse – as with Blueberry, it felt like we clicked. She had that same desire to please, and going out into an arena she had the same presence and bravery.

In May I also made my debut with Florentina, whom I'd bought back in 2012. For a while there had been a question mark over her because she was so bolshie when she was being backed. She'd knock you out of the way if you were on the floor with her, and even though she was a great mover, there's nothing you can do if the willingness to be ridden and trained aren't there.

Ryan Shannon, a good friend, was a great help in backing her, and when I finally got on her, I knew to my relief that my first impressions had been right and she was going to be a good one. After a few shows on her as a five-year-old, and with my hopes high, I decided to breed from her while she was still young and at the beginning of her career. Thanks to the Mount St John embryo transfer programme I could do that without disrupting her progress, and she now has a foal that's a half-brother to Blueberry, both of them being sired by Negro. The thought of another Negro horse to ride had huge appeal, but however good the bloodlines are, the end result whenever you breed from a horse is always slightly pot luck. Flora's colt came out like an absolute dream – he's jet black and officially called Limited Edition, although I call him Mowgli.

On both Flora and Freestyle it felt funny being back riding at little local shows. For a few years now the majority of my work had been at Grand Prix level with Blueberry, and although I was training my younger horses at home, I hadn't been out competing on them because I just hadn't had the time. The oddest thing was how leisurely it all felt: it's boom, boom, boom with movements in the Grand Prix, but at the lower levels I felt like I was just riding round in circles with all the time in the world. After riding in such big stadiums and in front of huge crowds, it did feel a bit as though I was back in the office, but even if the kick wasn't quite the same, there was still the thrill of developing a connection with a new horse.

* * *

There are very few competitions whose vibe I don't like, but going into the Europeans at Aachen in August

I was on edge. The experience I'd had there in 2014 was at the back of my mind, but I didn't want to think negatively – although I admit I was relieved to see we'd be in a different arena from the one we'd had the year before.

Michael Eilberg and Makarov were first to go for the team and made a mistake in the zigzag, but Fiona Bigwood on Atterupgaards Orthilia (Tilly), came back with 75 per cent, which was a great score. Carl was riding third and came out a little disappointed with his 75 per cent on Barney, so again Blueberry and I needed to pull in the big marks if we were going to get a podium place.

The supposed contest between Valegro and Totilas, which the media loved to hype up, was taking up a lot of space at Aachen. It still seemed ridiculous to me: there were seventy-two horses competing, so it was hardly a ride-off between the two of us. I was there to focus on my horse and do the best that I could, so even when it became clear that things weren't right with Totilas, it didn't make any difference to the way I felt when I rode into that arena.

So was it the memory of 2014 that was to blame for the mistakes I ended up making? Because I for one couldn't understand it: I'm normally so consistent, what the hell was going on? Why had I done it again? I made an error in the zigzag, which was ironic because I'd given Michael a lecture for doing the exact same thing, and also in the ones.

The result was that although I finished with the highest score, 83.029 per cent, it was less than one per cent more than Edward had scored with Undercover, so we went away with the silver and the Dutch went away with the gold.

I was so disappointed, but rather than wishing or hoping it was going to come right in the Special, I had to give myself a kick up the backside and go in fighting. I wanted that gold medal, and when Kristina Sprehe and Desperados came out with over 83 per cent it just made me hungrier. I set out with my mind made up that I was going out to get her and I did, coming back with 87.577 per cent.

Aachen had been a dramatic competition: Mathias and Totilas had withdrawn after the Grand Prix and Edward had been eliminated in the Special. Then Fiona was forced to withdraw Tilly, who had a sore back and a rash.

Nonetheless, the field for the Freestyle was still formidable with Kristina and Isabell Werth among the main contenders, and in a contest between the British and the Germans in Germany, it was obvious who the crowd were going to want to win.

By now, day four, Blueberry was beginning to feel tired and the humidity was taking its toll. Kristina and I were the last two riders to go, and as Blueberry and I were about to enter the arena, I saw her score of 88.804 per cent flash up on the electronic scoreboard.

That was enough of a distraction, but then the screens switched to live action and a camera operator suddenly zoomed in on Isabell, who had ridden earlier and was now eating an ice cream in the crowd. As her face appeared on the huge screen, everybody started laughing. 'Hello?' I thought. 'I'm trying to do a test here.'

The bell had rung, I'd put my hand up to start and all I could hear was the crowd laughing at Isabell. Somehow I had to focus and block it out, and although Blueberry was feeling increasingly fatigued and we again made mistakes in our changes, I came out feeling it had been good.

It's always a tense moment when you're waiting for your marks to be confirmed, but this was one of the most tense. My initial score was marginally ahead of Kristina's, but my marks then had to be sent to the Judges' Supervisory Panel to be assessed. The idea of the JSP is to correct errors and iron out the discrepancies that used to occur, but as the standard of judging has increased in recent years, marks nowadays rarely change by much. In this case, however, even the tiniest change could make all the difference.

As soon as I'd finished my ride there were people waiting to interview me, but I didn't want to speak to anyone until I knew. It was so close between me and Kristina. I can remember vividly sitting and waiting on Blueberry, thinking, 'Have I won? Have I not won?'

Then my marks were announced. I'd beaten Kristina but only just and as soon as my new score flashed up the crowd started to boo. It was the worst feeling: I'd only been doing my job, and I was being made to feel like I didn't deserve the win.

Carl had come fifth with Barney and we did a few interviews together, but by the time of the prize-giving Carl was getting ready to go home. I begged him not to leave me because I was petrified that I'd be booed when I went to get my medal, and I couldn't think of anything more horrible. I didn't know if I could face that.

As it turned out, the crowd booed the judges, but were generous enough to applaud when I stepped onto the podium. The seating was a long way back from the action, and for our lap of honour we'd been told to keep to the arena and not ride out on to the grass outside. Well, blow that – I wanted to interact with everyone who'd made the effort to come, so I cantered out of the arena and round the outside, waving and being clapped all the way. It hadn't been the greatest few days of my life, but it was a nice way to end them.

* * *

Blueberry was now twelve and a half and after Aachen some of the press suggested that he was beginning to show his age. Really all that had happened was we'd had a few blips and he'd been tired in the heat. At the end of the day, he's a horse like any other, but when you're so much in the spotlight everything gets blown up out of proportion.

Being subjected to that kind of scrutiny is just part and parcel of being at the top and it didn't affect the plans Carl and I had made: Blueberry had already had quite an intense year, so we decided that I'd take Uti to Olympia at Christmas and save Blueberry for Rio 2016.

Some horses need lots of competition practice and some don't, and Blueberry has always been the kind that doesn't. Barney, on the other hand, was the opposite: because he was such a spooky horse, he needed to be educated and reassured and gain confidence in the arena. In Barney's head there are always monsters lurking in corners or waiting in the flowerpots to get him, whereas that kind of thing never fazes Blueberry. He's always focused and always reliable, which meant that although we practised test exercises at home, all I really needed to do until the Olympics was to keep him happy and fit. Drilling him to the point of brain-deadness would have been counterproductive: I wanted him to be enjoying the moves and working because he wanted to, not because I was making him. When you force a horse, dressage starts to look ugly, not harmonious, and harmony is always the goal.

Meanwhile, life carried on and in September it was off to Stoneleigh as usual for the Nationals. As well as Freestyle and Flora, I was taking Barolo, a nine-year-old owned by Carl and Anne Cohn, in whom I also have a share.

Barolo had freaked out with me in the Prix St Georges at the 2014 Nationals, so how he'd cope in the Grand Prix I didn't know: if he was having a good day, I thought he stood a chance of winning, but he'd only done three Grand Prix before. British National Champion was one of the few titles I hadn't won, and Spencer had set the bar at 71.66 per cent, but Barolo defied my expectations and came out with 72.90 per cent. The next day we also won the Freestyle, which, given that Barolo had never done one before, was a tremendous achievement.

With Flora taking the Five-Year-Old Champion and Freestyle winning the Medium Open, I couldn't have been more pleased; I was also runner-up in the Four Year-Old-Champion with Mount St John Top Secret (Rosie). Rosie's another of Emma's horses and sired by Totilas, so she's quite small but very powerful.

Barolo lacked confidence in the arena but he had a lovely temperament, so in November 2015 Carl and I decided he was the right horse for a special job.

* * *

Cheltenham racecourse is just down the road from us here in Gloucestershire, and I had been asked to give a demonstration with the recently retired A. P. McCoy to mark the opening of its new Princess Royal Grandstand.

A. P. had won the Champion Jockey title twenty times but he still wanted to come and have a practice before the day, which was probably just as well: not only did I have to teach him how to sit down to canter, I also ended up giving him lessons in how to steer.

The skill that race-riding takes is phenomenal and A. P. is world-class, but his horses only ever have to go straight. Watching him try to make Barolo turn off the centre line as they were disappearing into the distance down the school, I had to stop myself from laughing – Barolo was clearly wondering what on earth was going on.

I'd decided that I was going to ride Pro-Set, Carl's retired Grand Prix horse, and my main aim on the day was to keep the two of us on the outside of the parade ring, so that when I turned, Barolo had no option but to turn too. A. P. was a great sport and we had a little go at piaffe/passage and a flying change in both directions, which A. P. turned out to be amazing at. But when I was asked if he might be a Rio contender, I had to confess I thought he still had some work to do.

* * *

I hadn't competed on Uthopia since May 2014, so when we headed off to Olympia in December I wasn't sure how it was going to work out. I needn't have worried: despite the big atmosphere it was like he'd never been away. In the Grand Prix our 77.46 per cent was just enough to keep Carl and Barney in second, but Granddad was out for revenge in the Freestyle.

Carl had come up with a floorplan that was about as difficult as he could make it, and he was also premiering new music from Tom Hunt that had a twenties and thirties feel.

Even with the degree of difficulty, he and Barney made it look effortless and their 83.75 per cent was untouchable. But if there's one person I don't mind coming second to it's Carl, and as he'd never won at Olympia before I couldn't have been more thrilled for him.

* * *

212

Even after London 2012, people would sometimes question whether dressage was a proper Olympic sport. It's not a comment that's ever been made to me directly, but my response would be this: if you think it's so easy, you should jump on and try giving it a go.

If you're a swimmer or a sprinter, all you have to concentrate on is perfecting your own performance; in equestrian sports, you also have to bring out the best in your horse. And although the oldest dressage rider at London 2012 was Hiroshi Hoketsu, who was in his seventies, it's physically demanding, too.

At the start of 2016, I was lucky enough to meet the cyclist Victoria Pendleton, who had retired after the London 2012 Olympics. She had decided to start a new career as a jump jockey, and was due to ride her first race at the Cheltenham Festival in March. When Victoria came to the yard to watch Carl and me ride one day, she confessed to me that she couldn't believe how hard it was: even though she was so fit, she was using muscles on a horse that she'd never had to use before.

Hearing how Victoria was building a new career for herself was fascinating, and I was delighted when she won her very first race. I don't think there's any way I'll still be competing myself when I'm in my seventies – I'd love to, but I suffer with my back as it is now. That said, as 2016 began, retirement was the furthest thing from my mind.

With the Olympics just eight months away, I wanted to make sure I was in the best possible shape. Since I'd started working with World Class I'd begun to get advice about my diet from a nutritionist, Julia Scott-Douglas, and although I'd been trying to eat healthily for years it was a real eye-opener. Often if I needed an energy rush I'd just reach for a chocolate biscuit: there were times when I'd literally be shaking if I hadn't had a sugar fix. What I hadn't understood is that sugar is like a rollercoaster: yes, you get a rocket high, but then your energy levels plunge.

Julia explained to me how nuts or a banana would give me much more long-lasting energy. She was pleased that I was already eating a good breakfast – porridge or brown bread or eggs, something that would set me up for the day – but less good was the fact I'd then drink endless cups of sugary tea, especially while trying to stay warm outside in the winter.

A few months earlier, Dean's dad had managed a ten-day grape and water detox. It sounded awful, but I wanted to get off the sugar so badly I was ready to give anything a go.

Day one was bad, day two was awful and day three was a complete, total nightmare. I couldn't believe I was feeling so bad and still standing up. It coincided with one of our pre-Olympic briefings: eight hours in a classroom learning about everything we could expect in Rio. All of it was good to know – what vaccinations we needed, how we were going to travel, how the horses were going to travel – but my head was pounding like you would not believe and all I wanted was to curl up under a desk. Then at lunchtime the sandwiches and biscuits came out, so I had to take myself off to my car for my grapes and water and some painkillers. I have to say, by day four I genuinely did feel amazing. I've stayed off the sugar since, too – although I do still love a good Rich Tea.

Blueberry's Olympic build-up began in February in Jerez: he wasn't competing, but as I was going to be away from England for two weeks I needed to keep up his training and fitness. Meanwhile, I introduced Barolo to his first international Grand Prix and Specials, which was a great success, yielding two seconds and a third.

The Hartpury Festival of Dressage, from 5–9 July, would now be Blueberry's only pre-Olympic outing, but in the meantime I had a packed schedule. All my up-and-coming horses had to be taken out to regionals so that they'd be qualified for the Nationals after I arrived back from Rio, and I also had my Olympic music to think about.

My floorplan was going to be the same as the one I'd put together for *How to Train Your Dragon*, but as with London 2012, I wanted music that would fit the place and occasion.

I'd seen the cartoon *Rio* and loved the jolly, uplifting carnival sound, so I asked Tom if he could come up with something similar. To begin with, I wasn't completely sure the theme would suit Blueberry: I thought it might be a bit too fast and lack the drama that emphasised the power and size of his movements. But Tom managed to capture everything I wanted although, as usual, it was down to the wire: my finished music didn't arrive until the afternoon of the Freestyle at Hartpury.

The team for Rio had been announced a few days before – there had only been three riders per team in London because of the sheer number of nations who wanted to take part, but four of us would be going to Brazil: me on Blueberry, Carl on Barney, Spencer on Supanova and Fiona on Tilly. And that was the way the four of us finished in the Grand Prix, scoring 83.28 per cent, 78.2 per cent, 77.5 per cent and 75.14 per cent. Then Carl scored a personal best, 79.215 per cent, with Barney in the Special, and Blueberry and I took the Freestyle with 90.63 per cent. Even though the Olympics were so close it was still business as usual: I had my whole string with me at Hartpury, so my Freestyle with Blueberry was actually my seventh test of the day.

Along with the spectators and cameras at Hartpury, I was being watched by a British journalist, Sam Knight. Sam was writing a long piece about me and Blueberry for the *New Yorker* magazine. I'd never heard of it before, so when I found out it was one of the most prestigious magazines in the world and had over a million subscribers, I was stunned.

Usually the people who interview me are quite knowledgeable about horses, and Sam had really done his research. The intensity of it was like nothing I'd ever encountered before: I'd be riding along and then he'd suddenly pop out from behind a hedge or round a corner with a whole new list of things he wanted to know.

Hartpury had been a good confidence boost for me and Blueberry, but I felt quite different in the build-up to Rio than I had done in the build-up to London. Before London I was literally ecstatic and jumping with joy; this time, I didn't want to get too excited. At the back of my mind I knew so much could still go wrong, plus it was such a long way for the horses to fly. The media coverage hadn't exactly filled me with enthusiasm, either: it seemed like every time you turned on the radio or TV there were stories about the facilities being terrible, or how we would all get the Zika virus.

World Class had done a great job in preparing us, warning us about the poverty we might see and how we could keep ourselves well and safe, but even as I was driving down to Heathrow with Carl and Dean it felt a bit like we might be on our way to the worst Olympic Games ever.

Of course, everything changed the moment we touched down.

13

A Golden Goodbye

ONE OF THE big worries, going into Rio, was that we wouldn't have anywhere to stay. The media was full of stories about athletes' accommodation not being ready and of the Olympic Village not being fit for habitation. An army of plumbers and electricians had been employed to go through the Team GB tower block and sort out any problems before we got there, and when we arrived we found absolutely everything had been done to make us as comfortable as possible, right down to the mattress toppers on our beds.

Not having stayed in the Olympic Village at London, I couldn't get over how like a holiday camp it felt: we had en-suite bathrooms; everywhere was kitted out with sofas and TVs, and there was food and drink laid on. The dressage team had somehow ended up with rooms on the top floor, and Fiona even had a penthouse with a jacuzzi and a balcony.

Up as high as we were the views were stunning: the mountains in the distance, then the Olympic Village spread out below. There were people everywhere, it didn't matter what time of day or night it was, and in all the time we were there the queue for the McDonald's never seemed to get any shorter. On the lowest floor of our tower there was a gym, ice baths and physio rooms, and I found it really interesting watching how people from different sports were being treated and strapped up.

Our horses had equally fantastic facilities, which was another relief. There was an air-conditioned indoor school, and each morning when we arrived at the stable yard our bus had to drive through disinfectant, then we had to walk through disinfectant ourselves, sterilise our hands and go through security scanners. Knowing that the Brazilians had gone to such lengths was very reassuring, and we felt that everything had been done to ensure we were able to perform at our best.

I'd been suffering with my back before Rio but Ash Wallace, who had taken over from Andy as our World Class physio, travelled out with us. Having her on hand to stretch me and open me up, give me acupuncture and strap me when I needed strapping, was another boost. Kate hadn't been able to come, but had told me I could call any time I needed her, even if it was the middle of the night.

I was glad of her support, but at the same time I didn't want to make Rio into something it wasn't. At the end of the day, it was just another competition: all that was different was that there were going to be more people watching than usual. Nerves were my worst enemy, so my plan was just to do what I do for every test, which is visualise myself going down the centre line at home, with Carl sitting at the bottom yelling at me to try harder. It always makes me so hungry I can't wait to get going.

How Blueberry would deal with the flights and the temperature was another matter. Alan had arrived with him a few days before to walk him out and get him acclimatised, but the first day I rode him things didn't go to plan: he was stiff from travelling and incredibly strong. I had Carl in my ear, telling me what to do, but what he was saying didn't feel right to me so I was trying not to listen.

Although it was hot, I knew that if I just kept playing with Blueberry and got him relaxed and listening to me we'd be fine. If I left it, as Carl was telling me to do, I'd come back the next day and Blueberry wouldn't be any better. I knew him so well that I just kept going, but that made Carl cross, and as soon as I got off he had a moan. 'You've got to listen to me, you're doing too much with him!'

'*You've* got to listen to *me*, because what it feels like and what it looks like are completely different! Do you want me to win a gold medal or not?'

'Stop stressing! Stop shouting at me!'

'I'M SHOUTING AT YOU BECAUSE YOU'RE NOT LISTENING TO ME!'

I swear, we're just like a married couple without the extra bits.

How Carl dealt with it all, I don't actually know. He was training all three of his team-mates as well as riding himself. I was quite worried for him at one point, wondering whether he'd be able to deliver with all the stress and responsibility.

The Grand Prix began on Wednesday 10 August, and both Fiona and Spencer nailed their tests. It was a particularly special moment for Fiona, who had to ride wearing an eye patch after a bad fall a few years before. She'd been nervous beforehand, even though she'd represented Britain at every level except Olympic, but as soon as she got out there on Tilly you wondered what she'd ever been worried about.

After the first day, Fiona was in third behind Germany's Dorothee Schneider and Sönke Rothenberger. Carl and I both felt the expectation that we'd deliver the following day, and Carl had been preparing Barney by trying to get him familiar with the arena. Unlike Blueberry, who can go into any atmosphere, Barney was still spooky, although since we'd arrived in Rio he hadn't really looked like he was worrying about anything.

I still couldn't watch them: I warmed Carl up, helped him with his final preparations, and then I walked away. It made me feel quite disloyal doing it, but I just can't watch Carl: my stomach churns and I get butterflies, plus I knew I had to focus and get myself into a good place for my own test a few hours later.

Unfortunately, Barney did have a spook – Carl joked that he'd tried to catch a Pokémon – and they came out with 75.529 per cent: disappointing, but not awful. Given that Kristina Sprehe and Dorothee Schneider had now both got over 80 per cent, though, it was going to be ridiculously tough to beat the Germans.

With the pressure upped even more, I knew that if I went out and did a good job, we could still get silver. 'Right, guys,' I thought, 'I'm going to do it.' Having all your team-mates around you is such a great feeling, and I was so much in the zone, all I wanted was to go and fight for it. Blueberry knew, too – I didn't even have to ask him for it, I just thought it. He would make me laugh sometimes because it was just as though he was reading my mind: I thought something and it happened. Maybe he was picking up on some kind of clue in my body, a slight shift of weight, but half the time when I rode him I felt like I was barely doing anything. Riding him was all about being light and sympathetic, and as long as you were he just gave and gave.

We came out with 85.071 per cent, which put us in the lead individually, and now that all of us had been in the arena once I thought there was a good chance we'd be better the next day for the Special. I hadn't ridden the Special test in full for over a year because of the demands it would place on Blueberry, but the Grand Prix had given me confidence and we started out well. Then we came around to do the trot half-pass and just as my outside leg came back, Blueberry's body hit my inside leg, which is the aid for canter. So, bless him, that's what he did. It was a split-second mistake and I knew I just had to forget it, but then we had a blip in our twos as well. As both movements are marked times two, they were expensive mistakes and we finished with 82.983 per cent.

It was funny when I came out of the arena: people thought I'd be disappointed or annoyed. And, yes, I was a little, but I didn't feel frustrated with Valegro at all. There's always a horrified reaction when he makes an error simply because he's so consistent – 'Oh my God! How do you feel? What happened?' – but he's a horse and I'm a rider and we make mistakes, although with Blueberry you can count them on one hand.

We'd all known that repeating the success of London would have been almost impossible at Rio unless everything had gone wrong for the Germans. Unlike in 2012, we didn't have the home advantage, and with Isabell, Dorothee and Kristina they had three riders who could hit an 80 per cent. Team silver was the medal we were really fighting for, and that was the one we ended up bringing home, with the United States taking the bronze.

I admit that I was a bit disappointed. The perfectionist in me wants to nail it every time out, and I hadn't done what I wanted to do. Fiona, who'd also made a few mistakes in her Special, felt a bit the same, so standing on the podium brought mixed emotions. But we'd all given it our best, every single one of us, and for me it had been a pleasure to ride with every one of my team-mates.

After that, it was time to catch up on some of the carnival atmosphere. Team GB had rented a house with a swimming pool and brought in caterers to throw a celebration barbecue for friends and family. Ben, Carl's partner, had the music blaring out, and everyone had quite a lot to drink: some of the owners were dancing round the pool pretending they were dressage horses.

It was quite funny, although getting to the point where you thought they should call it a day, but Carl was having a great time and was determined that I was going to join in. Before I knew what was happening, he'd grabbed me and thrown me, fully clothed, into the freezing, unheated pool. I was furious, as you can imagine, and what was worse was that I had my phone on me, which I never normally do. Usually I give it to Ian when I'm riding because I don't want to be distracted by messages, but just before leaving for the party we'd run into Andy Murray and ended up getting our photos taken with him.

Andy was sharing the other end of our floor back at the tower and as we were going out, we'd seen him sitting outside his room. He'd been locked out, so there he was, waiting, with all his little boxes of food stacked beside him: the really top, famous athletes often preferred not to eat in the Olympic Village food hall, just because it was so hectic and they were recognised all the time.

Ian, who was with me, couldn't believe it. 'Charlotte, there's Murray over there!'

'Well, go and speak to him then.'

'No, no! I can't do that.'

Ian's such a big fan that he was never going to do it himself, so I was going to have to do it for him. 'All right, Andy? What are you doing sat on the floor?'

After that, Ian and Andy were off – I think Andy had won his game that day, although I was just nodding my head and going along with it because I didn't really have much idea what either of them was talking about. Then Andy asked about our team, and I explained we'd just won silver, and also asked if we could have a picture. Andy graciously said yes, so Ian and I both got pictures on each other's phones, then left poor Andy waiting for someone to come with a key while we breezed off to our party.

Anyway – there I was in the pool, trying not to look like a bad sport because it was freezing: an August evening in Rio is still fleece weather. But Dean had seen Carl pushing me in and ended up pushing Carl in as well. After that Jane de la Mare, who owns Barney with Carl, also ended up in the water, followed by Ben. Carl thoroughly enjoyed himself and, wouldn't you know, only my phone got trashed: Carl had gone into the pool with his too, but he left it for a few days, turned it back on, and it started working fine.

The following days were like being on holiday: lovely weather, amazing scenery, running around on the beach. We found a little restaurant by the sea that we all liked and, although I'm not really a drinker, the mojitos they served there had me buzzing. We went to see Sugar Loaf Mountain and then we took a train up to Christ the Redeemer – even Fiona, who is scared of heights.

It's a long way up to that statue, and the view at the top is sensational: one moment you're lost in the clouds, the next they've cleared and you're seeing the city and the mountains and the ocean. It's like you're looking out over the whole world.

Carl had already told me that I was going to have to pray if I wanted to win a gold in the Freestyle, and I did – I'm not religious, but it's hard not to be moved when you're in a place like that and see the effect it has on everyone.

* * *

223

A lot had been said ahead of Rio about the Olympics being Blueberry's last competition. Carl was still keeping his options open when he talked to the press; he was finding it hard to say that enough was enough. Valegro was fit, healthy and on such good form that I think Carl would have liked to have kept going, but although I hadn't yet got a firm plan, I thought Rio could be the moment to draw a line. We'd done so much, won so much, it couldn't get any better – why keep going to the point where we started coming second or third? That, to me, wasn't what I was doing it for. Blueberry had given me more than I'd ever dreamed of and owed me nothing, absolutely nothing. I wanted him to finish at the top where everybody would remember him as the best horse there was. Yes, of course we could compete for another year and probably win some more gold medals, but why? The pressure and the expectation would keep building, and Blueberry didn't need that. I didn't want him finishing up as an older horse, not able to give what he used to, and open to all the criticism that would bring. Retiring him as the best was the right thing to do, but I wanted us to finish at the very top, and that was as Olympic gold medallists.

On the Monday morning, I went up to the stables to give Blueberry a pat and to take him out for a walk and some grass. Alan brought Barney, we were hand-grazing them and talking, and I said to Alan, 'If it all goes to plan and I win gold, I'm going to retire him after this.'

It was once I'd said it that the emotions started. Anders Dahl, Fiona Bigwood's husband, was riding for the Danish team, and in the stable yard he came over to me, touched my shoulder, and gave me a few words of support. Well, I literally had to bite my lip. The tears started rolling down my face and all I wanted to do was shut myself away. Everybody was wishing me luck, which was amazing, but I was an emotional wreck. I wanted so badly for it to go right. I took a little chair and went and put it in Blueberry's stable in the corner and just sat with him, crying. I didn't want anyone to speak to me, I didn't want anyone to see me, I just wanted to be with him.

Carl and I had worked out how we'd prepare: I'd do most of my warm-up in the air-conditioned indoor school while he was riding his test, and then we'd do the last minutes together in the ten-minute box to get Blueberry used to the heat. Team GB had an air-conditioned cabin on site equipped with physiotherapy beds, a kitchenette and beanbags, and after I'd had my physio with Ash I decided I'd stay there for a bit with Ian. We chatted about my music and my floorplan, but I must have been exhausted because I fell asleep. Ian, bless him, stayed with me the whole time, and when I woke up we put our music on and had our boogie, psyching ourselves up.

Then I walked out and the heat was like a smack in the face. It was over 30 degrees, no shade anywhere, and knowing how Blueberry was in the heat I instantly started to worry. But I had to deal with it – I couldn't change it, it was what it was, and I just had to do my best.

Ian watched me as we started warming up, and as soon as Carl had finished, he jumped off Barney and came to help. With ten minutes to go we went outside to do the final prep, and it was then that it hit me.

I could see down from the warm-up arena to where Kristina and Desperados were doing their Freestyle and hear their music playing. The nerves I experienced then were like nothing I'd ever felt before. Usually the bigger the competition, the more I want to get out there: bring it on. This time my heart was pounding through my jacket and my legs were like jelly. 'I can't feel my legs,' I said to Carl. 'I'm so nervous, I can't feel my legs.'

'You've got nothing to prove,' he said. 'You're going out there for yourself. Just go and enjoy it.' Even that was enough to make me want to cry. I had tears in my eyes when I walked Blueberry in the ten-minute box because I felt so nervous and worried and emotional.

Kristina's 87.142 per cent was enough to put her in first place. She was coming out but I still felt I needed more time. There was a slope down to the main arena, and as we all walked down it, Carl gave me a pat on the leg, and Dickie Waygood looked at me and said, 'Remember, it's the same shit, just another arena.' That's usually my philosophy too, but this time it felt completely different. Then Robbie Sanderson, who was a friend of Alan's and grooming for the German team, said, 'Go for it, girl.' And just like that the message got through. I picked myself up, held my head high, and as we came trotting round the outside of the arena it actually felt like Blueberry had taken hold of my hand. It was the most unbelievable feeling: like he was reassuring me and saying, 'We can do it.' From start to finish, he was perfect for me: it was the best feeling in the world. I was trying not to get emotional, but by the end tears were rolling down my face. It was one of the best rides of my life.

As soon as we finished I had my tack check then I was called for a doping test. Only after that could I get back to Blueberry, to cool him down in the indoor school. I walked him back with Alan, who was now also crying; Ian was jumping for joy, then Carl arrived, saw me and burst into tears. I think he'd been trying to be strong for me before my test, but I could tell he'd been worried: he knew how much I wanted it for that final ride.

I jumped off Blueberry and we were all crying and hugging each other: we'd been through so much together, put in so many hours and gone through thick and thin. Someone filmed Carl and me and put it on the internet, and watching it still makes me emotional now. Moments like that you just can't describe.

My 93.857 per cent had put me in first and I'd scored an artistic mark of 99 per cent, but Isabell Werth was the last to go. Then she scored 89.07 per cent and that was it: the ultimate dream, everything I'd ever wanted. To finish by delivering in that way – it was perfect. A perfect day and a perfect way for the fairytale to end.

* * *

After London, there'd been a huge anti-climax. It had been such a dream for me to get there, then all of a sudden I'd done it, won gold and it was all over. In 2012 I hadn't known where my career was going with Blueberry, or even if I'd be riding him in the future, and because I'd only been competing at Grand Prix for two years, I simply didn't have the knowledge and experience of how it all worked.

After Rio, it felt completely different. I'd had an amazing time, with a great team, and that individual gold had set the seal on the story. I also had the security of a string of exciting up and coming horses. My whole career to date had been spent with Blueberry, I'd learned everything with him all the way from the lowest level to the top, but I could now feed that experience into all the other horses I was lucky enough to be riding.

Just a month after Rio I went to the National Championships and won six different titles on six different horses. I didn't want to be thought of as a one-trick rider, and now I could show people what I'd been doing when I hadn't been on Valegro.

Winning the Advanced Medium on Freestyle confirmed for me that she is going to be my next star, and when I won the Prix St Georges with Carl and Ann Cory's Hawtins Delicato, we knew Del was shaping up to be Carl's. I also took the Medium title on Flora and the Novice on Mount St John VIP, a five-year-old whose elasticity and work ethic I'd loved from the first time I'd ridden her. To have such talented horses, and to work with such fantastic owners, makes me feel incredibly lucky, and it was great to be able to prove that it wasn't game over.

Blueberry had had such a light year competition-wise that when we got the chance to perform at the Central Park Horse Show in New York in September we thought, why not? It would be a nice opportunity for more people to see him and he loves performing anyway: the minute he hears crowds and sees cameras he turns on the showbiz.

The invitation to ride had come from Mark Bellissimo, who is the owner of the show. Mark had already invited me over for the 2015 show, when he'd come up with the idea that I ought to ride Frederick the Great. Frederick is a black Friesian stallion who is (apparently) the world's most handsome horse.

'He's got more likes than Valegro,' Mark kept saying.

'Oh, well,' I said. 'Swings and roundabouts, Mark. Blueberry's got more gold medals.'

I wasn't completely convinced, but Frederick was definitely a cool-looking horse and, being a Friesian, had mane down to the floor. I gathered up my reins and I was holding his hair, then I was riding with hair flying in my eyes and in my mouth: I felt like I was chewing on his mane half the time.

Mark is one of those people who can convince you to do anything, so when it turned out my trip also coincided with Pope Francis' 2015 visit to New York, Mark spotted another photo op. It was the craziest idea, but somehow he has a way of making things happen, so there was I posed on a horse while the Pope in his Popemobile drove along in the background.

Going back to New York in 2016 was just as much fun. The arena is constructed next to the ice rink where *Home Alone* was filmed, and with the city lit up at night it's like being slap-bang in the middle of all the New York movies you've ever seen.

For the first time, I was also going out on Blueberry without the pressure of being judged. I didn't have to think about competing against anybody, and although I wanted everyone to be able to see him at his best, he was there first and foremost to enjoy it and have fun.

Which he did: I could feel him loving every minute of it. It's almost as though he glows when he's being watched – he shines.

I'd said to Mark beforehand that it would be nice at the end if some of the people who'd come to watch could maybe meet Blueberry. Security is usually so tight, which is great, but it also means that people never get to see him up close. Mark agreed, but I hadn't quite realised what was going to happen, because all of a sudden there were people four or five deep around us, patting, stroking and trying to kiss Blueberry. I was doing autograph signings at the same time and it was crazy. There were a couple of security guards to keep us safe, but there was a sea of bodies all around us.

Many other horses would never have coped with a situation like that, but there was one moment when I looked up and it was almost as though Blueberry knew he had to divide his time between his fans. He'd been having selfies with all the people on his right-hand side, and then he turned his head so that he could say hi to everybody on his left-hand side. It was so funny to watch: he was completely working it, just like he does every time we walk out of the arena on a long rein. 'Yes, yes, hello, folks: it's me.'

Blueberry really is the kindest, kindest horse. Another date in 2016 was with the late Hannah Francis, who had founded the Willberry Wonder Pony charity after being diagnosed with bone cancer aged seventeen. Hannah had ridden all her life and it was one of her wishes to meet Blueberry, so although she was experiencing difficulty with the sensation in her legs, we put her up on him and Carl gave her a little lesson.

It was magical to watch. Sometimes, if one of the less experienced girls gets on Blueberry, he'll decide to have a bit of fun; with Hannah, it was as if he knew he had to look after her. By the end she was crying with happiness, Carl was crying, I was crying – there wasn't a dry eye left. And then she wrote me an amazing letter, thanking me for making her dream come true. She was such an inspiration, the bravest girl I've ever met, and meeting her was a privilege that will stay with me forever.

Olympia felt the right place for Valegro to say goodbye officially – it's a home show, one of the best in the world, and Carl and I both love it there. We had already both been invited to join a parade of the Rio Olympian and Paralympian Medallists, so as well as being reunited with Fiona and Spencer, we got to celebrate the success of Nick Skelton and the Paralympic dressage team of Lee Pearson, Sophie Christiansen, Sophie Wells, Natasha Baker and Anne Dunham.

I knew that making the farewell video was going to be emotional, but the first time that I saw the compilation of tributes to Blueberry that had come in, I couldn't speak. Tears were running down my face because although I already knew what a special horse he was, to hear it coming from so many other people's mouths was incredible. It really brought it home to me that this was it – after everything, we had finally come to the end.

When it came to my turn to record my segment, I had to keep getting the camera to stop because I was crying so much. In interviews people would ask, 'What would you say to thank Valegro?' and that was it, I was gone. How could you thank a horse that had done what he'd done for me?

Hearing my 2012 music again was another overwhelming experience: I loved it so much, and it made the hairs on the back of my neck stand up to relive all the memories of London. And yet the weird thing was that when I started practising it again, it felt so easy: in 2012 it had felt incredibly difficult, but with another four years' worth of experience, it was a breeze for both of us. It didn't feel hard at all. That was a measure of how far we'd come together.

By the time the night itself arrived, I'd managed to compose myself. I didn't want to be unable to answer questions when I was interviewed, and although I might have felt like I was losing Blueberry, I knew at the end of the day he'd be coming home with me, same as always.

Riding round the outside, with the cheering and thunderous clapping and the judges filming me on their iPads, sent shivers down my spine. I'd been a little worried in case it didn't go as well as I wanted, but from the moment the music started to the moment it stopped, Blueberry was absolutely sensational. The atmosphere, the buzz, the emotion … all of it brought tears to my eyes as I went down the centre line. 'What an incredible horse,' was all I could think.

When you ride an animal and you know they've given their all and there's nothing left – it's the most amazing feeling. Win or lose, it doesn't matter after that: what counts is that feeling, and that was the feeling Blueberry gave me every time. After every competition and every win, I'd always thought, 'Oh my God, how can this get better?' And we kept climbing and climbing, and every time it did.

For him to finish at his best, in front of all the people who loved him, was all I could ever have wished for.

14

Postscript

CHRISTMAS 2016 WAS the first time that I felt like I could actually draw breath in years. Until then, I was constantly living against the clock: if I wasn't riding, I was teaching or taking phone calls or doing photo shoots or being interviewed – it was never-ending. Finally I didn't have to rush or stress, I could spend time on the yard with the horses.

I'm so lucky to have incredible staff, but sometimes I miss doing the everyday stuff they do. It's not just when you're riding a horse that you build up a partnership with them; it's when you handle them on the ground.

With the yard quiet for the holidays I got to do everything myself again and I really, really enjoyed it. I love it when the horses recognise me: they start banging their doors and scraping the ground with their hooves because they know I'm coming with treats. Alan always moans about me making trouble but he enjoys it really, and it was so nice being able to work with him. I got to do the grooming; bathe the horses; tack them up; even do the mucking out again. It's such a satisfying job giving them a nice, cosy, fluffy bed: it's like tucking up a child. And it's also thinking time, when you can just be with your horse in the stable and talk to them while they nibble you and try and get you to scratch them or give them a carrot.

I had always planned that the year 2017 was going to be low key for me – the pressure and expectation of the last five years had been so intense, with people relying on me to deliver medals, that I wanted to take a step back. My main focus was on my horses coming through for 2018, when my aim is the World Equestrian Games in Tryon, North Carolina. Carl will be there with Hawtins Delicato, if all goes to plan, and I'm hoping to take Mount St John Freestyle. I'd also like to take another of my new horses, En Vogue, as a reserve.

I couldn't compete Vogue in 2016 because he was crazy. I bought him as a three-year-old and everyone decided I was mad, but I love proving people wrong and I thought he'd be an interesting project.

Vogue is by Jazz, and I'd always wanted a Jazz offspring – they're spooky, quirky horses, and generally very talented – but the first time I saw him in the stable at Sandra Biddlecombe's he was wild: he looked petrified of life. I think that was what made me want to buy him – I wanted to nurture him and convince him living wasn't that scary – but honestly, when I started lunging him and put the roller round his stomach, I thought he was going to explode. His head went straight up in the air and he wouldn't breathe.

Ryan Shannon breaks most of Sandra's horses, and he's brilliant at it because he knows just when he can safely get on their back. He doesn't use the most usual method: most people break horses in an indoor school, but Ryan takes them out on the road by the yard. Personally, if I was the one doing it, I'd want a soft landing, but his theory is that because the road is slipperier, horses don't want to buck as much there. 'OK, Ryan,' I thought as he went off with Vogue, 'if that's what you want to do …' But soon he was jumping on and off and Vogue didn't do a thing to stop him. It was incredible.

After that it was my turn to have a go and the moment I was on Vogue, that was it: I knew he'd be one of my favourite horses ever to ride. If I'd got on him and been scared he would have had a nervous breakdown, but because I got on him and made him feel as though he could do it, he believed me. Being able to give a horse that confidence and reassurance is an amazing feeling.

The biggest problem with Vogue ended up being that I thought he was black. After René I swore I was never, ever going to have a black horse again so I thought it might be a deal-breaker. Then I saw Vogue's horse passport: apparently he's 'donkey brown', so I could have him after all.

Another of my exciting new horses, Pumpkin (Gio), reminds me a bit of Fernandez: he's chestnut with a white blaze and the same beautiful neck. Like Dezzie, he's also tiny. I bought him after seeing him in LA, where I was teaching, and when I got him home and Carl set eyes on him for the first time, he turned round and told me I'd just bought a pony! There was a horrible moment when I wondered if that's what I'd actually done, because he did look very small when he came off the lorry. But when I rode him again I knew I'd been right to get him: like Dez, he's got the presence of a much bigger horse and that same cheeky character.

After 2016, everybody wanted to know what was going to happen next for Dean and me: in Rio, he'd stolen all the limelight by wearing a t-shirt with 'Can we get married now?' printed on it. I didn't see it until I was being interviewed after I'd ridden, and then the footage was played to me live on TV: Dean with his proposal, grinning from ear to ear.

Dean is the world's best supporter, and thanks to him we hit all the headlines. Both Reem Acra and Jenny Packham kindly offered to design me a wedding dress, but I personally don't feel as though a bit of a paper would change anything. Maybe we'll run away together and have a quiet little wedding somewhere, but I feel as though I'm pretty much married already.

Receiving a CBE for my performance at Rio was another huge honour for me. I went back to the Palace to collect it in March 2017, but I wasn't expecting anyone to recognise me because I was there with so many special people. It was fascinating learning about everybody else's lives and careers, but I didn't think anyone would have a clue about what I did until people started coming up to me. 'You're the girl on the dancing horse! My daughter loves you! She's going to be so jealous I've met you!' I couldn't believe so many people knew me and were interested, even down to the girl who did my hair and make-up beforehand. 'Oh my God! You ride horses! Oh my God! You've got a gold medal! *Oh my God!* You're getting a CBE!' Oh my God, she sounded just like I do.

I've had incredible recognition over the course of my career and genuinely feel completely humbled by it all. In Enfield there's even a 'Dujardin Mews', and after 2016 the local council decided to call one of its new blocks of flats 'Valegro'. Then in 2017 Carl and I were awarded the Spanish Riding School's Médaille de l'École d'Équitation Espagnole de Vienne, which is given to riders who follow the principles of classical horseman-ship. Princess Anne was at the ceremony, and afterwards Carl and I were invited to the Fête Impériale, which is the Spanish Riding School's summer ball and meant to be one of the grandest in the world. All the men were in black tie, and all the ladies were in beautiful dresses, and everyone arrived in horse-drawn carriages. Carl and I were making our way there, chatting between ourselves, and couldn't work out why everyone kept smiling and congratulating us as we were being driven through the streets. Then the penny dropped.

'Granddad! They think we've just got married!'

'Oh, well, Eddie – you've not done badly for yourself then, have you?'

I was also invited to make guest appearances on a new Netflix children's series, *Free Rein*, and the Sky sports comedy show, *A League of Their Own*. I nearly didn't agree to that one because I was so scared, but the other panellists included James Corden and so it was a once-in-a-lifetime opportunity. 'Come on, Charlotte,' I thought, 'you've got to do it. Push yourself out of your comfort zone.' Need I say it ended up being absolutely hilarious, and who'd ever have thought I'd one day be sitting on a pantomime horse that had Freddie Flintoff as its head and Jack Whitehall as its backside?

One of the lovely things about the position I'm lucky enough to be in is that it means I can give something back. In 2015 I became a Global Ambassador for Brooke, a charity that seeks to improve the welfare of working horses and donkeys (and the people who rely on them) in the developing world. It was important to me to know as much as I could about what Brooke did when I got involved – how they worked, who they helped – so I asked if I could join one of their trips to India in 2016. I was warned that I might find it upsetting, but I knew that even if I was going to be heartbroken, it was something I needed to do.

Alice Oppenheimer came with me and the night that we arrived in Delhi there was an earthquake. We were both a bit jet-lagged and exhausted with all that we'd been told and the safety advice we had to remember, so at first I wasn't sure if it was the bed shaking or if it was just me.

The next morning we visited one of the villages whose people are working with Brooke. Not everybody welcomes the animal welfare organisation because they worry that their working horses will be taken away from them, but one of Brooke's aims is to teach people how learning to look after their animals is actually in their own best interests: healthier, happier horses can do their work better. However, it isn't just the lack of money that's the problem in a lot of the places where Brooke works, it's also the lack of knowledge. What was great to see was how willing all the owners we met were to learn, and you could really tell the difference between communities that Brooke had visited and the ones they hadn't.

The hardest part of the whole trip for me was a visit to a brick kiln. The temperatures were over 40 degrees and bone-thin horses were struggling to pull carts piled up with hundreds of bricks. It was the saddest sight, and when you looked in their faces there was no life in them at all. When I see my horses and they see me, they light up and have a sparkle in their eyes, but with these horses there was nothing there.

Now, wherever I go, I try and talk about Brooke, because I was overwhelmed to see what they were doing. They help not just animals, but so many people as well. It's an amazing charity, and I feel privileged to be a part of their team.

Looking back at everything I've done, I often feel as though I'm the luckiest girl in the whole world. The people I've met, the places I've been, the opportunities I've had, and (of course) the horses I've been lucky enough to ride – it's almost unbelievable.

There have been so many occasions when I've been in the right place at the right time and everything has fallen into place for me, but I do also feel that I've worked my hardest and grafted to get where I am today. What I hope my story proves is that if you're dedicated and want something enough, even if people tell you it isn't possible, you can find ways and means of achieving it.

I owe so many thanks to everyone who's made my career possible: Debi, Ian, Judy, and especially my incredible mentor, Carl, who is an absolute joy and a pleasure to work with and who has inspired me in so many ways. I also wouldn't be where I am without my mum and dad: we've had our ups and downs, but they've backed me up one hundred per cent throughout my whole life. Their love and support enabled me to do what I've done, and it's been more than I ever dreamed of. With Valegro, I was able to make my very own fairytale come true – and now I can't wait for the next chapter to unfold.

Index

Index